ENDANGERED!
MAMMALS

For a free color catalog describing Gareth Stevens' list of high-quality books,
call 1-800-542-2595 (USA) or 1-800-461-9120 (Canada).
Gareth Stevens' Fax: (414) 225-0377.

Library of Congress Cataloging-in-Publication Data available upon request from publisher.
Fax: (414) 225-0377 for the attention of the Publishing Records Department.

ISBN 0-8368-1424-X

Exclusive publication in North America in 1996 by
Gareth Stevens Publishing
1555 North RiverCenter Drive, Suite 201
Milwaukee, Wisconsin 53212, USA

A LOVELL JOHNS PRODUCTION created, designed, and produced by Lovell Johns, Ltd.,
10 Hanborough Business Park, Long Hanborough, Witney, Oxfordshire OX8 8LH, UK.

Text and design © 1995 by Lovell Johns, Ltd. Additional end matter © 1996 by Gareth
Stevens, Inc.

U.S. series editor: Patricia Lantier-Sampon

Printed in the United Kingdom

1 2 3 4 5 6 7 8 9 99 98 97 96

ENDANGERED MAMMALS !

**WORLD CONSERVATION
MONITORING CENTRE**

Gareth Stevens Publishing
MILWAUKEE

CONTENTS

FOREWORD

Mark Collins, Director of the World Conservation Monitoring Centre.

In 1963, the IUCN Species Survival Commission, chaired by Sir Peter Scott, commissioned research and a series of books aimed at drawing to the attention of governments and the public the global threats to species. Sir Peter wanted more concerted action to address the problem of extinction. The first Red Data Book, published in 1969, was written by James Fisher, Noel Simon, and Jack Vincent. There had been earlier books that highlighted animals under threat and the possibility of extinction, the most important being written by G. M. Allen in 1942. The increasing threat to species and indeed our knowledge of these threats has resulted in nearly 6,000 species being listed as threatened in the most recent IUCN Red List of Threatened Animals. (IUCN uses different categories of threatened species, of which the most crucial category is Endangered.)

Knowledge of the conservation status of species is required so priorities can be set and management actions taken to protect them. The original Red Data Books were global assessments of species. However, many of these globally threatened species are found in only one country, and it has become increasingly important for each country to assess its own species and decide which should be listed as threatened. There are

Some of the many Red Data Books published since the first one appeared in 1969.

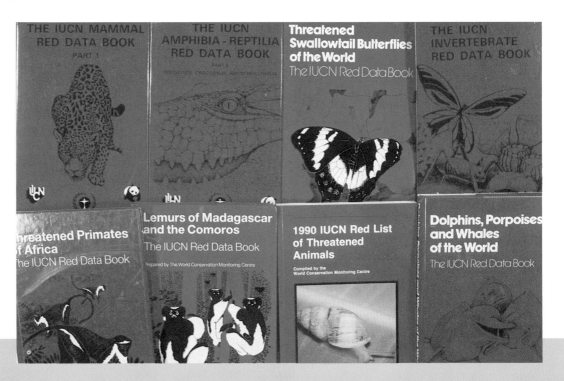

now many National Red Data Books covering substantial areas of the world.

The very fact that there are so many threatened species makes it very difficult to publish books on their status and distribution and, for some of them, we do not have detailed information. This *Endangered!* series aims to provide sound knowledge of 150 selected endangered animals and their natural habitats to a wider audience, particularly young people.

Our knowledge of threatened species can only be as good as the research work that has been carried out on them and, as the charts on this page show, the conservation status of much of the world's wildlife has not yet been assessed. Even for mammals, only about 55% of the species have been assessed. The only major group of which all species have been assessed are birds, and yet there are still large gaps in our knowledge of the status and trends in bird population numbers. However, their attractiveness and the interest shown in them by a great many people have improved the information available. Marine fish, despite their importance as a valuable food source throughout the world, tend to be assessed for conservation purposes only when their populations reach such a low point that it is no longer viable to catch them commercially. The 1994 IUCN Red List of Threatened Animals lists 177 endangered mammals representing 3.8% of the total number of mammal species and 188 birds representing 1.9% of the total number of species. Information on birds is compiled by BirdLife International.

The importance of identifying threatened species cannot be stressed enough. There have been many cases where conservation action has been taken as a result of the listing of species as endangered. The vicuna, a camel-like animal that lives in the high Andes of South America whose wool is said to be the finest in the world, was extremely abundant in ancient times but has been over-exploited since the European colonization of South America. By 1965, it was reduced to only 6,000 animals.

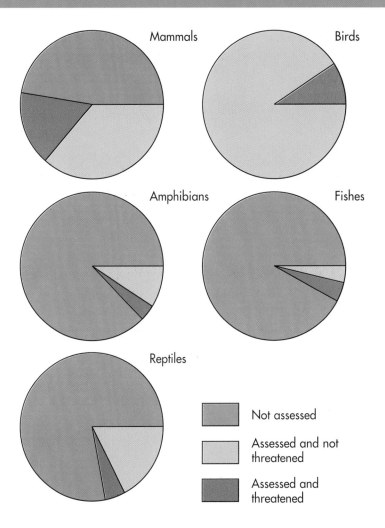

By protecting the vicuna from hunting and by establishing reserves, the population has steadily increased and is now in the region of 160,000. The vicuna is no longer an endangered species but is listed as Vulnerable. One high-profile endangered animal is the Indian Tiger, whose numbers had dropped to fewer than 2,000 in India when the first census was taken in 1972. Urgent conservation measures were taken, reserves were set up, and a great deal of expertise in their management has resulted in a population increase to its current level of about 3,250. Other measures included the halting of trade in tiger skins and other products such as bones and blood used in eastern traditional medicines. However, the other subspecies of tigers have not had this same protection, and their numbers are dwindling day by

day. Gray whales were also endangered. They migrate down the west coast of North America from arctic waters to the coast of Mexico and southern California to mate, returning for the rest of the year to feed and give birth to their young. Because their migration route was so well known, hunting was easy, and, as a result, their numbers had dropped to only a few hundred. Since hunting control measures began, the number of gray whales is now in excess of 21,000, and they are no longer endangered.

WCMC

The World Conservation Monitoring Centre at Cambridge in the United Kingdom has been the focal point of the management and integration of information on endangered plant and animal species for more than fifteen years. WCMC's databases also cover the trade in wildlife throughout the world, information on the importance and number of areas set up to protect the

world's wildlife, and a Biodiversity Map Library that holds mapped data on many of the world's important sites and ecosystems. It was IUCN, through its Species Survival Commission, that first established the World Conservation Monitoring Centre as its information database for species and ecosystems. WCMC now carries on this role with the support of two other partners: the World Wide Fund For Nature and the United Nations Environment Programme.

IUCN — The World Conservation Union

Founded in 1948, The World Conservation Union brings together states, government agencies, and a diverse range of nongovernmental organizations in a unique world partnership: over 800 members in all, spread across some 125 countries. As a union, IUCN seeks to influence, encourage, and assist societies throughout the world to conserve the integrity and diversity of nature and to ensure that any use of natural resources is equitable and ecologically sustainable. The World Conservation Union builds on the strengths of its members, networks, and partners to enhance their capacity and to support global alliances that safeguard natural resources at local, regional, and global levels.

Various organizations too numerous to mention help countries protect their wildlife. We urge you to support these organizations so the list of endangered species does not continue to grow. Your voice will be added to the many millions who are urging international cooperation for the protection and wise use of the wildlife that is such an important part of our natural heritage.

Headquarters of the World Conservation Monitoring Centre, Cambridge, England.

Like the platypus, the two species of echidnas are monotremes, or egg-laying mammals. The long-beaked echidna lives in the mountains of New Guinea in cloud-blanketed, damp forests at altitudes of 3,280 to 9,840 feet (1,000 to 3,000 meters). Its habits are not well known, but scientists believe it is nocturnal and eats mainly earthworms and some insects. The female lays a single egg that is incubated in a pouch on her belly.

The long-beaked echidna needs a large home range, but its population density is low, only four animals per square mile (2.59 square kilometers). This means it can easily be extinguished from a particular area.

Echidnas are regarded as a delicacy and are often hunted with specially trained dogs. Some parts of their range have also been destroyed by logging, farming, and mining. The total population was estimated at 300,000 in 1974. The species, however, is now extinct in large areas of the Central Highlands of New Guinea, especially where the human population is dense, and has declined in many others. The echidnas are still relatively common in remote forests.

Echidnas are fully protected in Irian Jaya but can still be hunted by traditional methods in Papua New Guinea. However, effective conservation will require more reserves to protect known populations of echidnas. Education about the echidna's situation will also need to be increased.

FACTS

SCIENTIFIC NAME: *Zaglossus bruijni*

RED DATA BOOK: Endangered

AVERAGE FULL-GROWN SIZE:
Total length 19-30 inches (47-78 centimeters)

FULL-GROWN WEIGHT:
11-22 pounds (5-10 kilograms)

LIFE SPAN: 30 years

The long-beaked echidna is a rare, egg-laying mammal found only in New Guinea.

The numbat is a unique marsupial equivalent of an anteater. Its diet consists of termites, and it only rarely eats ants or other insects. Unlike most marsupials, the numbat is active by day, spending its time looking for termite nests. When it has found one, it burrows in and licks up the termites with its long tongue. A captive numbat eats 10,000 to 20,000 termites every day.

The numbat once ranged across southern and central Australia, but it now lives only in a small area of southwestern Australia. Since Europeans arrived in Australia, the numbat's range has decreased by 90 percent. It lives in eucalyptus forests, where there are hollow logs for shelter and termites to eat.

Numbats are mainly solitary and live in large territories of about 370 acres (150 hectares), but males and females sometimes share territories. Females give birth to four young in grass-lined burrows. Numbats do not have pouches like many other marsupials, but the young fasten themselves to their mother's breasts.

The numbers of numbats have been reduced by destruction of their forest homes for agriculture, changes in forest management that make the forests less suitable for numbats, and predation by introduced European red foxes and cats. A recent major decline is probably due to an increase in foxes and a long drought.

Numbats are being conserved by protecting the remaining eucalyptus forests and by transferring numbats to new areas where foxes have been controlled. There are now three populations, and more are being established.

FACTS

SCIENTIFIC NAME: *Myrmecobius fasciatus*

RED DATA BOOK: Endangered

AVERAGE FULL-GROWN SIZE:
Head and body length 69-108 inches (175-275 cm)
Tail length 51-67 inches (130-170 cm)

FULL-GROWN WEIGHT:
9.7-16 ounces (275-450 g)

LIFE SPAN: Not known

The numbat is active during the day, which is rare for marsupials.

Like several other Australian species, Leadbeater's possum was once believed to be extinct but was rediscovered in the 1960s. The first specimen was found in 1867, and only another four specimens were found by 1909. No others were spotted until 1961. The species was probably never widespread, and it is now confined to the tall, open forests in the Central Highlands of Victoria, Australia.

These forests are dominated by three kinds of acacia trees: mountain ash, shining gum, and alpine ash. The possums need large trees over 150 years old that, living or dead, can provide hollows for the possums to inhabit. They live in groups of up to eight that include one breeding female, one or more mature males, and their offspring. A large nest is made in a hollow to provide insulation during the winter. An undergrowth of shrubs and young trees provides insects and plant gums for the possums to eat.

The specialized requirement for old trees with hollows makes Leadbeater's possum very vulnerable to habitat destruction. Fires and clear-cutting of the forests destroy the habitat. Even if the trees are allowed to regrow, it takes 150 years before Leadbeater's possums can reestablish themselves.

Some protection is provided by reserves, but experts predict the species will continue to decline. Leadbeater's possums are currently being bred in captivity, but if wild trees in their natural habitat continue to be destroyed, it will take a long time for the forests to regenerate to their original state.

Leadbeater's possum is particularly vulnerable to habitat destruction, since it lives in hollows in large acacia trees. If cleared, it takes 150 years for these trees to regrow to the right size.

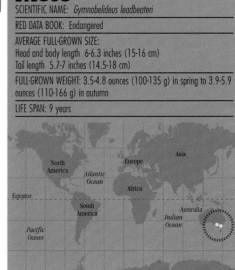

FACTS

SCIENTIFIC NAME: *Gymnobelideus leadbeateri*

RED DATA BOOK: Endangered

AVERAGE FULL-GROWN SIZE:
Head and body length 6-6.3 inches (15-16 cm)
Tail length 5.7-7 inches (14.5-18 cm)

FULL-GROWN WEIGHT: 3.5-4.8 ounces (100-135 g) in spring to 3.9-5.9 ounces (110-166 g) in autumn

LIFE SPAN: 9 years

RYUKYU FLYING FOX

The Ryukyu flying fox is a fruit bat found on many of the Ryukyu Islands of southern Japan, Taiwan, and some surrounding islands. Within this range, there are five subspecies on different groups of islands. They are all endangered because of their small populations.

Fruit bats are long-lived and slow-breeding. Some, in fact, have lived as long as thirty years in captivity. Females do not give birth until one or two years of age, and they bear only a single young at a time. Such slow-breeding animals are especially vulnerable to disasters, especially when the population is small, because they are slow to recover. Catastrophic destruction of habitat and animals by a typhoon or cyclone is, therefore, a serious threat. The populations on the Daito Islands, which number no more than fifty bats on each, must be at special risk, but there are larger populations on Iriomote and some other islands.

Ryukyu flying foxes already suffer from a continuing loss of habitat. The forests they roost in during the day and feed in during the night are being destroyed, along with the figs they eat. They can, however, exploit fruit crops and are pests on plantations. Flying foxes are also hunted for food on Kashoto Island in Taiwan.

The Ryukyu flying fox is protected as a national monument by the Japanese government, and the handling of flying foxes is regulated on Kashoto Island. The species does not occur in any reserve; therefore, the conservation of food plants and roosting sites may be the best means of preservation.

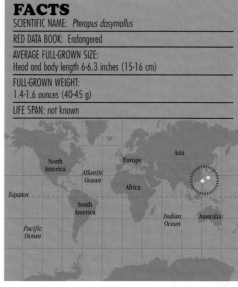

FACTS

SCIENTIFIC NAME: *Pteropus dasymallus*

RED DATA BOOK: Endangered

AVERAGE FULL-GROWN SIZE:
Head and body length 6-6.3 inches (15-16 cm)

FULL-GROWN WEIGHT:
1.4-1.6 ounces (40-45 g)

LIFE SPAN: not known

Most populations of Ryukyu flying fox are very small and at risk from both natural disasters and habitat destruction.

GHOST BAT

The fierce-looking ghost bat is frightened of humans.

The current population is 4,000 to 6,000, and it is declining. One roost that numbered 450 bats in 1960 dwindled to 150 by 1976. The bats roost singly or in small groups for most of the year, but they gather in single-sex colonies during the breeding season. These groups usually number fewer than 100, but there is a roost of 1,500 in the Kohinoor gold mine at Pine Creek, Northern Territory.

Bat roosts are very sensitive to disturbance, and human intruders cause the bats to become anxious and leave. This will be more of a problem as remote areas are opened up for tourism. Also, many cave roosts have been destroyed by mining and quarrying, or are threatened by mining proposals. On the other hand, the bats make use of abandoned mine shafts.

The ghost bat is protected by law from being collected or killed. Unfortunately, the law is not enforced properly, and there is no protection for the roosts except for the few that occur in reserves.

Also called the Australian false vampire, the ghost bat is the only Australian member of a family that occurs in Africa and Asia. These bats are carnivores that hunt prey ranging from large insects to lizards, frogs, birds, and mammals — and even other bats. Remains at ghost bat feeding sites show that their main prey are mice, budgerigars, and owlet-nightjars.

The ghost bat has a scattered distribution in Western Australia, the Northern Territory, and Queensland, where its habitat ranges from arid country to lush rain forest. It must once have had a wider distribution because sub-fossil remains have been found much farther south. The decrease in range may have been due to the climate becoming drier.

GREATER MOUSE-EARED BAT

Thirty years ago, the greater mouse-eared bat was common throughout much of Europe and the Middle East, from the Baltic Sea to Syria and Israel. Since that time, its numbers have decreased enormously, and it has become virtually extinct in northwestern Europe and Israel. In the late 1940s, there were huge colonies of greater mouse-eared bats in the Netherlands, but they almost disappeared by 1970. In Poland, a single colony of three thousand in a church has also disappeared. The species was never common in the British Isles, where it was last spotted in 1990.

Greater mouse-eared bats live in open, wooded country, where they hunt for large moths and beetles. They are in decline because of the increased use of insecticides that are killing their food source and also because of the loss of pasture where they live. The bats use large buildings and caves for roosts, especially for nursery colonies in summer. Such places are easily disturbed and are often destroyed completely. The largest numbers of bats are often in those caves that are most likely to be disturbed.

Bats are protected by law in most European countries, and deliberate persecution is not often a problem today. However, loss of roosts and feeding grounds continues to cause problems. It is sometimes possible to guard cave roosts with grills, but education about the need to protect bats is necessary. New roosts have been created successfully in Germany and the Netherlands.

FACTS

SCIENTIFIC NAME: *Myotis myotis*

RED DATA BOOK: Vulnerable

AVERAGE FULL-GROWN SIZE:
Head and body length 2.6-3.2 inches (65-80 millimeters)

FULL-GROWN WEIGHT: .7-1.8 ounces (20-45 g)

LIFE SPAN: 13 years

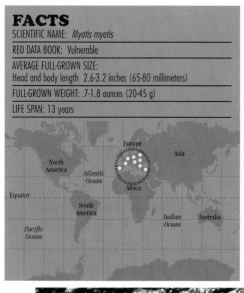

Carnivorous greater mouse-eared bats feed on moths and beetles.

GOLDEN BAMBOO LEMUR

First discovered in 1987, the golden bamboo lemur was immediately granted endangered status because it was recognized to be one of the most threatened lemurs in Madagascar.

Its habitat is rain forest with plenty of bamboo, especially the giant bamboo. Bamboo leaves are the primary food of the golden bamboo lemur. The young shoots it prefers are rich in protein as well as toxins that are poisonous to most other mammals. This lemur lives in small family groups of two to six individuals. Each group has a territory of about 200 acres (80 ha), and the lemurs appear to be active mostly by day.

The golden bamboo lemur is restricted to an area of forest centered around the village of Ranomafana, which was made a National Park in 1991, and in the Andringitra Strict Nature Reserve. It probably lived in other areas before the forests were cleared for agriculture.

The golden bamboo lemur population, estimated at one thousand in the Ranomafana National Park, lives mainly in reserves. All lemurs are protected under Malagasy law, but the law remains difficult to enforce.

FACTS

SCIENTIFIC NAME: *Hapalemur aureus*

RED DATA BOOK: Endangered

AVERAGE FULL-GROWN SIZE:
Total length Males 29 inches (74 cm); females 31.7 inches (80.5 cm)

FULL-GROWN WEIGHT: 3.3 pounds (1.5 kilograms)

LIFE SPAN: Not known

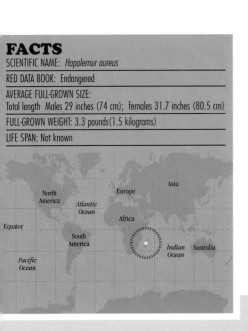

The golden bamboo lemur feeds on the tender shoots of the giant bamboo, a food that is poisonous to other mammals.

The lemur family is confined to the island of Madagascar. Its survival depends on the safeguarding of suitable habitat. Its forest home has been experiencing a massive loss due to agricultural development. The ruffed lemur's range is in the eastern rain forests, where small groups of two to five individuals live in fiercely defended territories. It feeds mainly on fruit, with small amounts of nectar, seeds, and leaves.

Although there are no estimates for the size of the population, it is clear that it is declining. As well as losing their habitat, ruffed lemurs are commonly kept as pets in Madagascar and are even exported. This trade is a major cause of their decline in some areas.

All lemurs are protected in Madagascar, although the law is difficult to enforce. The ruffed lemur is found in a number of reserves, and there are two subspecies. The black-and-white ruffed lemur is widely distributed, but the red ruffed lemur is confined to the Masoala Peninsula, where there are no protected areas.

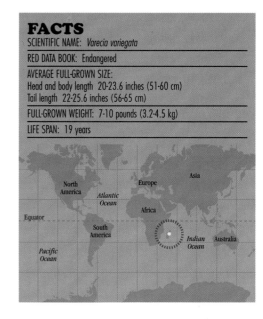

FACTS

SCIENTIFIC NAME: *Varecia variegata*

RED DATA BOOK: Endangered

AVERAGE FULL-GROWN SIZE:
Head and body length 20-23.6 inches (51-60 cm)
Tail length 22-25.6 inches (56-65 cm)

FULL-GROWN WEIGHT: 7-10 pounds (3.2-4.5 kg)

LIFE SPAN: 19 years

The red ruffed lemur is the rarest of the ruffed lemurs.

AYE-AYE

This unusual member of the lemur family was thought to be almost extinct, but it is more widespread than originally suspected. Aye-ayes live in rain forests, deciduous forests, dry scrub forests, and coconut plantations. The original range was throughout northern, northwestern, and eastern Madagascar.

The aye-aye is solitary and nocturnal, spending the day in treetop nests. It has a unique method of feeding on insect grubs by excavating holes in rotten wood with its large incisor teeth and pulling out the grubs with its long middle finger. It uses the same technique for eating the flesh of hard-skinned fruits.

The main threat to the aye-aye is the destruction of its forest home for timber and agriculture. It is also killed because it raids crops and because of local superstitions that it brings bad luck.

The species survives in several national parks and reserves, although protection is lacking. It has also been introduced into the Nosy Mangabe Special Reserve, an island off the north of Madagascar, and it has been bred in captivity. Even if enough of the aye-aye's habitat can be preserved, education of local people will be needed to back up legal protection. Farmers should also be compensated for loss of crops.

The aye-aye, a nocturnal lemur, may be more widespread in Madagascar than scientists once thought. However, it is still an endangered species.

FACTS

SCIENTIFIC NAME: *Daubentonia madagascariensis*

RED DATA BOOK: Endangered

AVERAGE FULL-GROWN SIZE:
Head and body length 14-17 inches (36-44 cm)
Tail length 19.7-24 inches (50-60 cm)

FULL-GROWN WEIGHT: 4.4 pounds (2 kg)

LIFE SPAN: over 23 years

GOLDEN-HEADED LION TAMARIN

FACTS
SCIENTIFIC NAME: *Leontopithecus chrysomelas*

RED DATA BOOK: Endangered

AVERAGE FULL-GROWN SIZE:
Head and body length 7.9-13.4 inches (20-34 cm)
Tail length 12-15.8 inches (31-40 cm)

FULL-GROWN WEIGHT: 21-28 ounces (600-800 g)

LIFE SPAN: 15 years or more

Golden-headed lion tamarins are still captured as pets, even though they are a protected species.

The four species of lion tamarin are among the most strikingly colored of all mammals, and they are all endangered. They live in the rain forests on the Atlantic coast of Brazil. This was the first part of Brazil to be settled by Europeans, and only a few fragments of the original forests remain.

Tamarins live in small groups of two to eight individuals, although they sometimes gather into larger groups of fifteen or sixteen. They are monogamous and usually give birth to twins. The tamarins' diet consists mainly of fruits and insects, but they also eat lizards, birds, and eggs.

The golden-headed lion tamarin was always restricted to the state of Bahia, and there were no more than 550-600 individuals left in the wild in 1990. About 400 of these were in the Una Biological Reserve, which extends over 17,300 acres (7,000 ha). However, the habitat continues to disappear at a rate of about 5 percent per year, and the reserves are occupied by hundreds of human settlers.

The attractive appearance of golden-headed lion tamarins and other lion tamarins makes them a collectors' item and has led to a trade in live animals. At one time, hundreds were exported legally, and an illegal trade flourished even after they had been granted protection. In a period from 1983 to 1984, fifty to sixty golden-headed lion tamarins were exported to Belgium and Japan.

Captive breeding is an important part of the conservation of the lion-headed tamarin. In 1993, there were 575 individuals held in forty-nine institutions. Breeding is regulated by the breeding program and studbook of the International Committee for the Recovery and Management of the Golden-headed Lion Tamarin, which is supported by the Lion Tamarins of Brazil Fund. Survival of the species in the wild will depend on proper protection of their environment and the success of the education program in Bahia.

Muriqui is the name given to this monkey by the Tupi Indians of Brazil. It is also called the woolly spider monkey. This is the largest monkey in the Americas, and it is also the most endangered.

Spider monkeys can hang from branches by their tails, and they rarely descend to the ground. Their food consists of leaves, flowers, and fruit.

Muriquis live only in the rain forests that once stretched along almost the entire Atlantic coast of Brazil. Most of these forests have been destroyed, and muriquis now survive only in the remaining patches. The forests have been cut down for fuel and timber or for human farm settlements. Muriquis have also been hunted for food or captured as pets.

There are now only 700 to 2,000 muriquis left. They live in groups of twenty-five or more animals.

Muriquis are found in about twenty-three reserves, but many may be too small to support strong populations. Survival of the species is being helped by a captive breeding program at the Rio de Janeiro Primate Centre. This program started with two pairs of adults in 1990, and the first birth was in 1991. Six muriquis have now been born at the center, and four of them survive.

Muriquis spend virtually their whole lives in trees, where they feed on leaves, flowers, and fruit.

FACTS

SCIENTIFIC NAME: *Brachyteles arachnoides*

RED DATA BOOK: Endangered

AVERAGE FULL-GROWN SIZE:
Head and body length 18-24.8 inches (46-63 cm)
Tail length 25.6-31.5 inches (65-80 cm)

FULL-GROWN WEIGHT: 26-33 pounds (12-15 kg)

LIFE SPAN: Not known

A close cousin of the baboon, the drill is found from the Sanaga River in southern Cameroon to the Cross River in southeastern Nigeria, and also on the island of Bioko. It lives only in forests and not in open country. It cannot, therefore, survive deforestation.

Drills live in groups ranging from a dozen to nearly two hundred individuals. Units of a dozen or so females exist within these groups, with a single male that is twice their size. The drills spend much of their time on the ground, feeding on fruit and invertebrate animals.

There has been very severe forest clearance in Cameroon. Even where the native forests are replaced by plantations, the drills are driven out because they cannot feed on eucalyptus or other exotic trees.

Drills have also suffered from hunting. In 1975, experts estimated a level of hunting high enough to seriously threaten the survival of species in the wild.

There is still a viable population of drills in the Korup Reserve in Cameroon, a protected area that contains drills. It is not known whether there are viable populations elsewhere.

Young, orphaned drills are cared for at the Drill Rehabilitation and Breeding Centre in Nigeria. Elsewhere, drills have remained in captivity for at least two generations. In 1992, there were forty-three in captivity.

There may be only one viable population of drills left in the wild.

FACTS

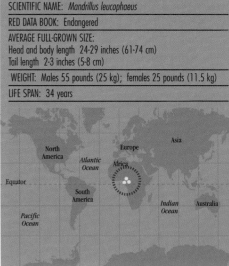

SCIENTIFIC NAME: *Mandrillus leucophaeus*

RED DATA BOOK: Endangered

AVERAGE FULL-GROWN SIZE:
Head and body length 24-29 inches (61-74 cm)
Tail length 2-3 inches (5-8 cm)

WEIGHT: Males 55 pounds (25 kg); females 25 pounds (11.5 kg)

LIFE SPAN: 34 years

The Chinese government is making considerable efforts to safeguard the golden snub-nosed monkey.

FACTS

SCIENTIFIC NAME: *Pygathrix roxellana*

RED DATA BOOK: Vulnerable

AVERAGE FULL-GROWN SIZE:
Head and body length 22.5-30 inches (57-76 cm)
Tail length 20-28 inches (51-72 cm)

FULL-GROWN WEIGHT: 35 pounds (16 kg)

LIFE SPAN: Not known

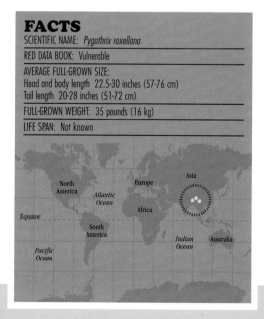

The golden snub-nosed monkey is one of three snub-nosed monkeys living in China. All three are threatened with extinction. The golden snub-nosed monkey lives in southern China, neighboring parts of Tibet, and possibly Assam, India. There are about 10,000 to 15,000 of these monkeys in existence.

The golden snub-nosed monkeys are found in high mountain forests up to about 11,155 feet (3,400 meters), but they descend to lower altitudes in winter. They live in troops of 100 to 600 animals. Each troop is made up of families consisting of one male, about five females, and their offspring. They spend most of their time in trees but sometimes come to the ground to eat or play. Their food consists of tender pine and fir needles, bamboo shoots, fruit, berries, nuts, and bark.

The destruction of their forest homes is the most serious threat to the golden snub-nosed monkeys, but hunting is also a serious problem. Their meat and bones are used for traditional medicines, and their skins are also valuable. The long back hair is used to make coats. Sometimes whole villages hunt these monkeys. They are also captured because some zoos pay high prices for such unusual animals.

The Chinese government has made the golden snub-nosed monkey a high priority for conservation. The Zhouzhi Nature Reserve of 386 square miles (1,000 sq. kilometers) has been set up specially for this species. Since it lives in the same habitat as the giant panda, it will also benefit from many of the reserves set up to protect the panda. The Chinese government is trying to stop hunting by teaching offenders about the importance of animals and by fines or prison sentences.

FRANÇOIS' LEAF MONKEY

The leaf monkeys of southern Asia are related to the langurs. The François' leaf monkey lives in the moist forests of southern China, northern Vietnam, and eastern Laos as far as the Mekong River. The river, in fact, forms the western boundary of the species range. At one time, it ranged farther east into China and Hainan Island.

François' leaf monkeys live in troops of one adult male, four to six females, and their offspring. They feed on leaves and some flowers and fruits. When the weather is cold, the monkeys take shelter for the night in caves, and the species' range is associated with rocky areas and limestone hills with caves.

This animal is being threatened by the destruction of forest habitat by logging, harvesting fuel wood, and agriculture, and because of hunting for food and medicinal purposes. In addition, François' leaf monkey suffered in the heavy bombing during the Vietnam War.

Fewer than twenty-five thousand François' leaf monkeys survive. Little is known about their precise distribution and habitat requirements, but more reserves are needed within the species' range. There are six or seven subspecies, all of which will need conservation.

FACTS

SCIENTIFIC NAME: *Trachypithecus françoisi*

RED DATA BOOK: Endangered

AVERAGE FULL-GROWN SIZE:
Head and body length 19-26 inches (48-67 cm)
Tail length 32-35 inches (82-89 cm)

FULL-GROWN WEIGHT: 16.7-19.8 pounds (7.6-9 kg)

LIFE SPAN: 28 years

The habitat of the François' leaf monkeys was badly damaged during the Vietnam War.

HOOLOCK GIBBON

Hoolock gibbons live in small, monogamous groups that consist of a male, a female, and up to three offspring of different ages: infant, juvenile, and subadult. The gibbons have a varied diet of fruit and leaves, but they also eat insects, eggs, and small vertebrate animals.

The hoolock gibbons' habitat ranges from evergreen rain forests to semi-evergreen forests to mixed forests to hill forests. They once lived across much of south-eastern Asia and could be found throughout the region from India and Bangladesh to Myanmar and southern Yunnan, China.

The gibbons have decreased through rapid deforestation and hunting practices that have not included any conservation measures. Two-thirds of the original forest has now disappeared. In Assam, India, for instance, forests have been replaced largely by tea plantations. Slash-and-burn agriculture by hill tribes and commercial logging have also destroyed forests. One result of forest clearance is that the gibbons have to descend to the ground from their tree habitats to cross clearings and roads. This makes them more vulnerable to predators and hunters. They are intensively hunted for meat in Assam, and in Yunnan their meat and bones are used as a tonic in traditional medicines.

The world population of hoolock gibbons is probably around 170,000, but some national populations are small. Fewer than 200 live in Bangladesh, and only 100 to 200 in Yunnan. Some populations live in national parks, such as those in Blaphakram and Namdapha in India, but scientific study of the species' ecological requirements are needed so that effective reserves can be created or existing ones improved. In Yunnan, stronger legislation is needed, especially in reserves where it should be illegal to carry firearms or other weapons used to kill protected species.

The hoolock gibbon's traditional forest habitat is being destroyed through much of its range.

FACTS

SCIENTIFIC NAME: *Hylobates hoolock*

RED DATA BOOK: Endangered

AVERAGE FULL-GROWN SIZE:
Head and body length 17.7-25.6 inches (45-65 cm)

WEIGHT: Males 12.3 pounds (5.6 kg); females 12 pounds (5.5 kg)

LIFE SPAN: Not known

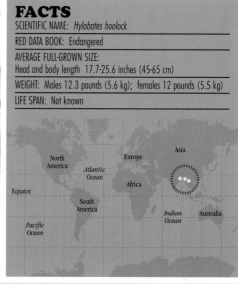

GORILLA

Gorillas live in two regions of Africa: equatorial western Africa and east central Africa, which are separated by 620 miles (1,000 km) of the Congo tropical forests. Gorillas prefer the edges of tropical rain forests, regrowing forests, and bamboo forests. Few live in primary forest.

Gorillas live in small groups of one adult male, two to four adult females, and two to five immatures (less than eight years old). The groups do not hold territories, but they do stay away from each other. Only lone males live outside the groups. Gorillas living in western Africa eat mainly leaves, and those in eastern Africa eat more fruit, but all gorillas have a varied diet.

There are three subspecies of gorilla. The population sizes of gorillas are not known accurately, but the western and eastern lowland gorillas are estimated at 35,000-45,000 and 3,000-5,000 respectively. The mountain gorilla, which lives only in an area 25 miles (40 km) long and a few miles (km) wide, numbers only 400-450. It is possible that the western lowland gorilla is a species separate from the others.

The range of gorillas has decreased in many countries, and the animals are now extinct in some areas. The decline has been mainly due to forest destruction and hunting. Poaching has been a problem in some reserves.

The survival of the gorilla depends on preserving their forest habitat and preventing hunting. In some places, such as the Virunga National Park, Rwanda (where mountain gorillas live), and in Zaïre, gorillas are being conserved by tourism. Groups of gorillas become tame enough for visitors to see them at close quarters. Money from the tourists helps to pay for the guards and management of the reserves. Unfortunately, gorilla tourism in Rwanda has been disturbed by the recent civil war. The war has threatened continued conservation of the Virunga gorillas.

FACTS

SCIENTIFIC NAME: *Gorilla gorilla*

RED DATA BOOK: Vulnerable

AVERAGE FULL-GROWN SIZE:
Head and body length, when standing erect 4-5.7 feet (1.25-1.75 m)

FULL-GROWN WEIGHT:
Males 298-606 lbs. (135-275 kg); females 154-309 lbs. (70-140 kg)

LIFE SPAN: Not known

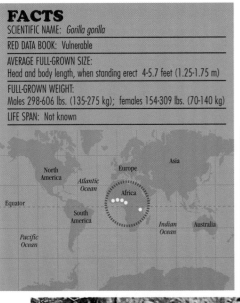

Vulnerable mountain gorillas live only in small areas of Rwanda and Zaïre.

PYGMY CHIMPANZEE

The total wild population of the pygmy chimpanzees is uncertain since they live in just a few locations in the forests of Zaïre.

FACTS

SCIENTIFIC NAME: *Pan paniscus*

RED DATA BOOK: Vulnerable

AVERAGE FULL-GROWN SIZE:
Head and body length 27.6-32.7 inches (70-83 cm)

FULL-GROWN WEIGHT:
Males 81.5-135 pounds (37-61 kg); females 60-84 lbs. (27-38 kg)

LIFE SPAN: Not known

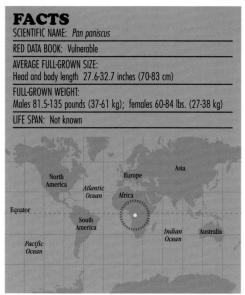

The pygmy chimpanzee, or bonobo, was recognized as a separate species by a study of museum specimens in 1929. Even then, not all zoologists accepted that there were two species of chimpanzee. The pygmy chimpanzee is not much smaller than a common chimpanzee.

Pygmy chimpanzees are found only in the forests of Zaïre, south of the Zaïre River. Although there are large areas of forest where the species might live, it is limited to a few small locations. It is not known how many pygmy chimpanzees exist.

Unlike their close relatives, pygmy chimpanzees frequently stand upright. They live in nomadic groups of thirty to eighty individuals, but these sometimes split up into parties of six or more to forage, or they combine into larger groups. Females mature at ages 13 to14, and they give birth every 3 to 7 years. The chimpanzees' diet consists mainly of fruit, but they also eat seeds, leaves, invertebrates, and sometimes small mammals.

Until the 1970s, pygmy chimpanzees were safe in the dense forests, but human settlement has expanded, and the forests are being cut for timber. The only place the chimpanzees can live alongside humans is at Wamba, where local tradition is that pygmy chimpanzees and humans were once brothers. Elsewhere, pygmy chimpanzees are hunted for food and for traditional medicines. Because the chimpanzees flee into the trees, they are easy to shoot. Babies are captured by killing the mothers and are sold as pets or to zoos and medical laboratories.

Although the animals are protected, the law is not enforced, and there are not enough reserves where the pygmy chimpanzee is safe. The Salonga National Park was set up to protect the species, but few pygmy chimpanzees live there. A Bonobo Protection and Conservation Fund has been set up to help the species.

CHIMPANZEE

The chimpanzee is now seriously endangered or extinct in many parts of its former home range. It once had a wide, discontinuous range through equatorial Africa in a variety of habitats from rain forests to deciduous forests to dry savanna woodlands.

Within this range, chimpanzees live in communities of twenty to one hundred animals, averaging about thirty-five. They eat fruits, flowers, and seeds, together with young leaves and a number of small animals.

Chimpanzees once inhabited twenty-five countries, but they are now extinct in five (Gambia, Guinea-Bissau, Burkina Faso, Togo, and Benin). They will probably become extinct soon in Ghana, Nigeria, Burundi, and Rwanda. Only ten nations have more than 1,000 chimpanzees, and the largest populations live in Gabon, Zaïre, Cameroon, and perhaps Ivory Coast. There are about 200,000 chimpanzees living in the wild, but many populations are small and in danger of disappearing.

Threats to chimpanzees vary from region to region and include habitat loss, hunting, and the capture of infants for the pet, entertainment, and biomedical trades. Civil wars have led to increased hunting and the occupation of reserves by refugees. Despite legal protection throughout its range and a listing in Class A of the African Convention, law enforcement is usually poor or nonexistent. The Committee for the Conservation and Care of Chimpanzees, an international nongovernmental organization, is producing action plans for each country to identify conservation goals. Success, however, depends on the stability of these nations.

The chimpanzee is already extinct in many countries.

FACTS

SCIENTIFIC NAME: *Pan Troglodytes*

RED DATA BOOK: Endangered

AVERAGE FULL-GROWN SIZE:
Head and body length 25-37 inches (63.5-94 cm)
Height when standing 3.28-5.6 feet (1-1.7 m)

FULL-GROWN WEIGHT:
Males 75-154 pounds (34-70 kg); females 57-110 pounds (26-50 kg)

LIFE SPAN: Maximum in wild may be 50 years

ORANGUTAN

FACTS

SCIENTIFIC NAME: *Pongo pygmaeus*

RED DATA BOOK: Endangered

AVERAGE FULL-GROWN SIZE:
Height when standing 4-4.9 feet (1.25-1.5 m)

FULL-GROWN WEIGHT:
Males 318 pounds (144 kg); females 143 pounds (65 kg)

LIFE SPAN: 50 years

Trade in orangutans is one of the major threats to the future of the species.

The orangutan is found only on the islands of Borneo and Sumatra, with a different subspecies on each. It is the largest tree-dwelling mammal and, unlike the chimpanzee and gorilla, it spends nearly all of its time in trees. It lives in the rain forest, from sea level to altitudes of 5,900 feet (1,800 m).

Orangutans are solitary animals. The females spend only a few days at a time with a male when ready to mate. The single offspring spends up to ten years with its mother, who gives birth about once every six years. Each orangutan travels slowly through the forest, spending many hours feeding on durians, litchis, mangoes, and other fruits, as well as leaves, insects, and, occasionally, small birds or mammals.

Orangutan fossils have been found far beyond their present range, in Java, northern Vietnam, and southern China. The species probably once inhabited all of south-eastern Asia.

Most of the Sumatran subspecies live inside the Gunung Leuser National Park, while the Bornean subspecies can still be found over much of Borneo except Brunei-Darussalam. The majority live in Kalimantan, where large areas of forest remain.

As well as the destruction of their forest homes, orangutans have suffered enormously from the trade in live and dead animals. It has been estimated that up to one thousand orangutans were imported into Taiwan between 1991 and 1994; five or six die for each one that arrives alive. Taipei, the capital of Taiwan, is said to hold more orangutans per square mile (sq. km) than the species' native forests. The trade will be difficult to stop because of the profit to be made from an orangutan, which ranges from $6,000 to $15,000.

Orangutans are protected by law, but enforcement must be improved. Existing reserves need better protection, and new ones should be organized. Attempts are being made to return illegally captured orangutans to the wild.

GRAY WOLF

The gray wolf was the world's most widely distributed mammal before rats, mice, and other species were carried around the world by humans. It lived throughout the northern hemisphere, north of 51° N. This range has been greatly reduced, and the wolf is extinct over large areas. It is now confined mainly to remote wilderness areas. It has disappeared in many areas of the United States, Asia, and most of Europe except the eastern section. The world population is estimated to be 124,775 to 135,625 animals, with the largest single population of 50,000 in Russia. Numbers are very patchy; the wolves are abundant enough to be pests in some places, while they are near extinction in others. The Mexican wolf, a subspecies, had been reduced to less than ten animals in the wild in 1990.

Wolves usually live in packs and have a complex social system. Only the dominant pair in the pack breeds. Packs usually consist of eight to twelve animals, but sometimes as many as thirty. Their diet is varied. Packs cooperate to hunt moose, caribou, and other deer, and they attack domestic livestock. They also eat carrion, small mammals, and nesting birds.

Wolves have always been persecuted. They are viciously portrayed in fairy tales, and there is a belief that they attack humans. Packs of wolves need large areas for hunting, and fragmentation of their habitat makes it difficult for viable populations to survive. The species is also in danger because of interbreeding with dogs.

Although protected in many parts of its range, hunting continues in many places where the law is not enforced. However, the gray wolf breeds well in captivity, and many are held in zoos. There are also plans to reintroduce the wolves in some areas where they have become extinct.

The gray wolf lives in packs in remote wilderness areas.

FACTS

SCIENTIFIC NAME: *Canis lupus*

RED DATA BOOK: Vulnerable

AVERAGE FULL-GROWN SIZE:
Head and body length 39-60 inches (100-150 cm)
Tail length 12-20 inches (31-51 cm)

FULL-GROWN WEIGHT:
35-132 pounds (16-60 kg)

LIFE SPAN: 16 years

RED WOLF

The red wolf became extinct in the wild and survived only because of a captive breeding program.

The red wolf once lived in the lowland swamps, bushlands, and forests of the southeastern United States, from southern Florida to Texas. It is very similar to the gray wolf, but smaller and tawny in color, and may have been the gray wolf's ancestor. The social system is similar, with the red wolf living in packs that are primarily family groups. Its prey includes swamp rabbits, coypus, raccoons, and small deer.

The red wolf has suffered because of hunting and habitat destruction. Vast wetland areas were drained for agriculture, while dams flooded more habitat. At the same time, private individuals and government organizations killed red wolves in predator control programs. Interbreeding with coyotes also reduced the red wolf population. By 1980, the red wolf was extinct in the wild.

A number of red wolves, however, had been kept in captivity, and a captive breeding program was established at Point Defiance Zoological Gardens, Tacoma, Washington. In 1988, red wolves were reintroduced to the wild in the Alligator River National Wildlife Refuge in North Carolina. By 1991, their numbers had grown to thirty and there are now over two hundred in captivity.

Further reintroductions into reserve areas are planned, but education about the true, harmless nature of the red wolf is needed to reduce persecution of these animals by humans.

During the nineteenth century, the Ethiopian wolf lived in most parts of Ethiopia, but its population has declined throughout this range because the land is being used for agriculture. Elsewhere, there has been a general degradation of its habitat, which has reduced the numbers of its prey. Overgrazing by sheep, for instance, reduces the food available for the rodents that the wolves prey on. At the same time, the wolf has been persecuted as a predator of sheep, while interbreeding with dogs reduces the purity of the species.

The Ethiopian wolf is now restricted to moorlands in the Arssi, Bale, Simien, and other mountain ranges. The total population is under 1,000 individuals, and the only local population of any size is in the Bale Mountains National Park, where there are an estimated 500 to 600 wolves. Like other wolves, Ethiopian wolves live in packs that consist of about seven wolves. The largest group on record was seven adults and six pups. The wolves usually forage alone by day for small mammals that can range from hares to grass rats.

The Ethiopian wolf is protected by law, and local populations are protected in the Bale and Simien National Parks, but this protection needs to be more effective. Saving the species in the wild will not be easy, but a program has begun. A survey of remote areas is discovering the locations of surviving pockets of animals that need protection. There are no Ethiopian wolves in captivity, and a breeding program needs to be established to help build up the species stock. Hybrid wolves and dogs should probably be removed from the wild population.

Only one sizeable population of Ethiopian wolves remains in the wild.

FACTS

SCIENTIFIC NAME: *Canis simensis*

RED DATA BOOK: Endangered

AVERAGE FULL-GROWN SIZE:
Head and body length 39.4 inches (100 cm)
Tail length 13 inches (33 cm)

FULL-GROWN WEIGHT: Males 33-40 pounds (15-18 kg); females 28.6-35 pounds (13-16 kg)

LIFE SPAN: Not known

WILD DOG

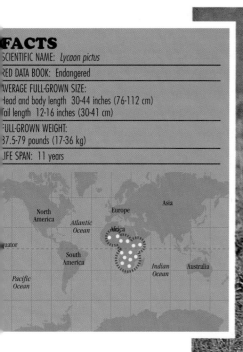

A wild dog feeds young members of the pack.

The wild dog, sometimes referred to as the African hunting dog, could once be seen in much of Africa, from southern Algeria in the north to Namibia, Botswana, and northern South Africa. It prefers savanna woodland, open plains, and forests, but can sometimes be seen in the Sahara Desert and the mountains. There has been an alarming decline recently in the wild dog population. It is probably extinct in sixteen countries it once inhabited, and is rare in others. The largest remaining populations are in the eastern and southern regions of Africa, but the total population is only between 2,000 and 5,000.

Wild dogs live in packs composed of several related adult males and several females from other packs. The size of the pack ranges from two to twenty, but only the dominant male and female mate. Their pups are fed by all the adults. The pack hunts cooperatively, and the dogs can kill large mammals such as greater kudu, zebras, and wildebeest.

The rapid decline of the wild dogs has occurred for several reasons. They are persecuted by farmers, they suffer from diseases such as distemper and rabies, and their habitat is disappearing. Each pack needs a huge hunting range; for example, packs on the Serengeti Plain, in Tanzania, have ranges of 580 square miles (1,500 sq. km). As human populations expand and the habitat is fragmented by agriculture, the wild dog is driven out. Its disappearance is hastened by poisoning or shooting despite legal protection in many countries. The species survives in marginal land that is no good for farming, such as very dry country and wetlands. Healthy populations are likely to remain only in large reserves such as the Serengeti and Kruger national parks. There is also a plan to reintroduce wild dogs to the country around Mkomazi, Tanzania.

IBERIAN LYNX

The Iberian lynx of Spain and Portugal is similar to the species of lynx that ranges across northern Europe, Asia, and North America, except that it is smaller. Both species have been persecuted for centuries, but the Iberian lynx's small range has made it more vulnerable to extinction. It is the most endangered carnivore in Europe.

The Iberian lynx lives in forests and the type of habitat called maquis. This is open countryside of heather and other low shrubs. The lynx is solitary and nocturnal, and it preys almost entirely on rabbits.

At one time, the Iberian lynx was found throughout Spain and Portugal, wherever there was suitable habitat. It disappeared from the Pyrenees in the 1950s and is now found only in parts of central and southwestern Spain and in nearby parts of Portugal. The remaining population of about one to two thousand are separated into small groups of lynxes.

The Iberian lynx is hunted for its skin and because farmers are afraid it will attack their livestock. The lynx has also disappeared because its habitat has been converted to farmland or tree plantations. Only 2 percent of the original range is now suitable for lynxes. In places where they live, many lynxes are caught in traps set for rabbits and foxes, or they are run over by cars.

It is difficult to set up large reserves in a rapidly developing country, so the plan to save the Iberian lynx involves linking protected areas and reintroducing captive-bred lynxes into suitable parts of their old range.

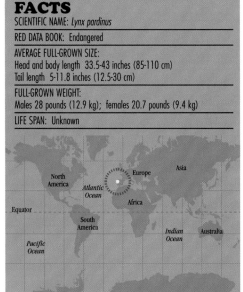

FACTS

SCIENTIFIC NAME: *Lynx pardinus*

RED DATA BOOK: Endangered

AVERAGE FULL-GROWN SIZE:
Head and body length 33.5-43 inches (85-110 cm)
Tail length 5-11.8 inches (12.5-30 cm)

FULL-GROWN WEIGHT:
Males 28 pounds (12.9 kg); females 20.7 pounds (9.4 kg)

LIFE SPAN: Unknown

The Iberian lynx is found only in limited parts of Spain and Portugal and is Europe's most endangered carnivore.

CLOUDED LEOPARD

FACTS

SCIENTIFIC NAME: *Neofelis nebulosa*

RED DATA BOOK: Vulnerable

AVERAGE FULL-GROWN SIZE:
Head and body length 24-41.8 inches (61-106 cm)
Tail length 21.7-35.9 inches (55-91 cm)

FULL-GROWN WEIGHT:
35-51 pounds (16-23 kg)

LIFE SPAN: Up to 17 years

The clouded leopard's distinctive markings make its pelt popular with poachers.

The clouded leopard is interesting to zoologists because it is a link between the big cats (lion, tiger, leopard) and small cats. Unlike the big cats, the clouded leopard cannot roar. Its habitat is mainly rain forests, but also open forest, scrub, and mangroves. It lives in trees where it hunts monkeys and birds or drops onto deer and wild boar. Because the clouded leopard is a solitary and elusive forest dweller, little is known about its habits.

At one time, the clouded leopard was found over most of southeastern Asia, from Nepal and Sikkim to southern China and Taiwan, south through Myanmar, Thailand, Indochina, Malaysia, Borneo, and Sumatra. As the rain forests have been destroyed, it has become rarer, and it is believed to be near extinction in Nepal and Taiwan. However, because the clouded leopard is not well known and is difficult to study, it can only be assumed that it is vulnerable to extinction. Both the extensive loss of habitat and hunting for its pelt, teeth, and bones (which are used in Asian medicines) are contributing to the plight of the clouded leopard.

The clouded leopard is protected by law over most of its range, and a captive breeding program has been set into action.

One hundred years ago, tigers could be found from eastern Turkey and the Caspian Sea across Asia to eastern Siberia and south to the Indonesian islands of Sumatra, Java, and Bali. Now they survive only in pockets of this range. Tigers have a wide range of habitats that include rain forests, mangrove swamps, grasslands, savannas, and mountain country. Only deserts and high mountains are without tigers.

The original population of tigers was around 100,000, but there are now between 5,000 and 7,400. Of the eight subspecies of tiger, the Indian tiger is the most abundant, with 3,250-4,700 left in the wild. The South Chinese tiger is down to 30-80 individuals, and the Caspian, Javan, and Bali tigers are extinct.

Tigers are solitary except when courting and rearing cubs. Litter size is usually two or three. The cubs are striped and remain with the mother until about the second year, when they can kill prey on their own. Males have home ranges of up to 38.6 square miles (100 sq. km) that include the smaller ranges of several females.

The disappearance of the tiger has been due to the loss of its habitats, which is made worse by the loss of its prey — mainly deer, antelopes, wild pigs, and buffalo. Big game hunters used to shoot large numbers of tigers, and today many of these animals are deliberately poisoned by farmers to protect their livestock.

There is also a trade in tiger skins and bones, blood, and other parts of the body that are used in traditional medicines. International trade in tiger products has been banned, but it still continues. A single tiger is worth as much as $60,000. In 1994, the United States introduced trade sanctions against Taiwan to stop importation of tiger products. In 1993, about 1,100 pounds (500 kg) of tiger bones were confiscated in New Delhi.

Two major tiger conservation projects exist today. Project Tiger in India has created eighteen tiger reserves, the centers of which are kept clear of human settlement. The first reserve was opened in 1973, and since then the number of tigers has doubled. In 1994, eleven countries in the tiger's range set up the Global Tiger Forum. The forum hopes to set up more reserves and stop the use of tiger products.

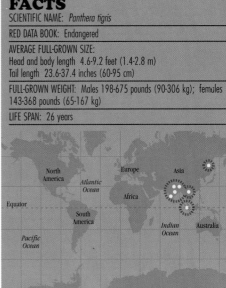

FACTS

SCIENTIFIC NAME:	*Panthera tigris*
RED DATA BOOK:	Endangered

AVERAGE FULL-GROWN SIZE:
Head and body length 4.6-9.2 feet (1.4-2.8 m)
Tail length 23.6-37.4 inches (60-95 cm)

FULL-GROWN WEIGHT: Males 198-675 pounds (90-306 kg); females 143-368 pounds (65-167 kg)

LIFE SPAN: 26 years

The tiger's distinctive fur marking is a major factor in the tiger skin trade.

FACTS

SCIENTIFIC NAME: *Uncia uncia*

RED DATA BOOK: Endangered

AVERAGE FULL-GROWN SIZE:
Head and body length 39.4-51 inches (100-130 cm)
Tail length 31.5-39.4 inches (80-100 cm)

FULL-GROWN WEIGHT:
55-165 pounds (25-75 kg)

LIFE SPAN: 19 years

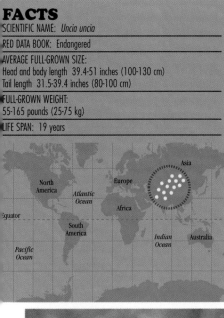

The solitary snow leopard lives in rugged, remote parts of Central Asia.

The beautiful snow leopard lives in the mountainous areas of Central Asia that cover the countries of Russia, Kazakhstan, Kyrgyzstan, Mongolia, China, Afghanistan, Pakistan, India, Nepal, and Bhutan. Its preferred habitat is dry shrubland or grassland with steep gullies, cliffs, and rocky outcrops. Not surprisingly, it has been difficult to study an animal that lives in such a rugged terrain in remote places. Yet this has not deterred hunters from seriously reducing the snow leopard's numbers.

The snow leopard is solitary except when pairs are courting and females are accompanied by their cubs. Its prey is wild sheep and goats, but also includes smaller animals such as pikas, hares, marmots, and gamebirds.

Snow leopards have been placed in jeopardy by overhunting of the large hooved animals that are their main prey and also by large-scale poisoning of pikas and marmots to protect crops. When snow leopards try to replace the loss of their natural prey by killing livestock, they come into conflict with humans and are killed.

Snow leopards used to be hunted for their fur, which was in great demand in the fashion trade. Although the fur has disappeared from the international market, a few snow leopard coats are still for sale in China and Taiwan. One pelt is worth more than sixty times the minimum yearly wage in Kyrgyzstan. There is also a demand for snow leopard bones in the Chinese medicine trade.

Snow leopards are currently found in over one hundred reserves, but some of these are large enough to support no more than a few pairs. Attempts are being made to enlarge protected areas of snow leopard habitat and to conserve the species in settled land by compensating farmers for loss of their animals. It is also necessary to enforce protection laws and regulations on international trade in snow leopards. China and India have conservation projects. The Indian Project Snow Leopard is similar to the Project Tiger and provides money for reserves.

BLACK-FOOTED FERRET

The black-footed ferret has returned twice from apparent extinction. It once lived across the Great Plains of North America, from Alberta, Canada, to the southwestern United States. Two hundred years ago, it lived in twelve states, but by the 1950s it was believed to be extinct. Then a colony was discovered in 1981 at Meeteetse, Wyoming. Disaster struck this colony in 1985 when canine distemper killed many of the animals. The remainder were captured and kept in captivity.

Black-footed ferrets live only in and around prairie dog towns, which include huge colonies of these burrowing rodents. The ferrets live in the prairie dogs' burrows and prey on them, although they also eat other rodents, birds, and insects. A large expanse of prairie with plenty of prairie dogs is required to support a population of black-footed ferrets. It takes 100-150 acres (40-60 ha) of prairie dog town to support one black-footed ferret. As farmers and ranchers exterminated prairie dogs to save the vegetation for their livestock or plowed the land and planted crops, the black-footed ferret became rare, and its populations were split up. And, although the prairie dogs once thrived in large numbers on the open plains of North America, 97 percent of their habitat has disappeared.

The Meeteetse population of black-footed ferrets was being carefully protected, and its numbers were increasing until it was infected by distemper. In 1985, only twenty-five black-footed ferrets remained in existence. However, the captive animals bred well and, by 1992, they had increased to 349. In 1991, forty-nine were released in Wyoming, and another reintroduction has since been made in Montana.

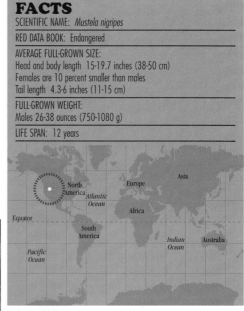

FACTS

SCIENTIFIC NAME: *Mustela nigripes*

RED DATA BOOK: Endangered

AVERAGE FULL-GROWN SIZE:
Head and body length 15-19.7 inches (38-50 cm)
Females are 10 percent smaller than males
Tail length 4.3-6 inches (11-15 cm)

FULL-GROWN WEIGHT:
Males 26-38 ounces (750-1080 g)

LIFE SPAN: 12 years

Black-footed ferrets live in and around prairie dog colonies.

The giant panda, symbol of the World Wide Fund for Nature, is still endangered in spite of worldwide interest in the species.

The giant panda is the symbol of the World Wide Fund for Nature (WWF). Although today it is familiar and popular, little was known about the species in the wild until recently. Zoologists are even undecided whether the giant panda belongs to the raccoon or bear family.

At one time, the giant panda was distributed over a large part of southeastern Asia, from Myanmar and Vietnam through southern and eastern China, as far north as Beijing. Its range has declined because of changing climate and an increasing human population. Giant pandas are now restricted to six mountain ranges in central China. The present population is only about one thousand; the largest single population is seventy pandas living in the Woolong Reserve in Sichuan.

The giant panda habitat is bamboo forests growing at heights of 8,860 to 12,800 feet (2,700 to 3,900 m). The animals eat young bamboo shoots almost exclusively, but they sometimes eat grass, bulbs, and small animals. Giant pandas are solitary, and females give birth to one to three cubs but may attempt to rear only one.

Giant pandas are hunted for their pelts. Although this practice is illegal, high prices encourage poachers to take the risk. Clearing bamboo forests for agriculture is a more serious threat. The giant pandas' habitat in Sichuan Province was reduced by half between 1974 and 1989.

This problem is made worse because giant pandas need to eat bamboo. Bamboo plants flower once and die. One important species of bamboo died out during the 1980s, and many pandas died of starvation. At one time, the pandas would have traveled to find a new source of bamboo, but this is not possible with so little habitat left.

The Chinese government and WWF are trying to conserve the giant panda by increasing the number of reserves and also by protecting pandas living outside reserves. This will cost approximately $50 million.

FACTS

SCIENTIFIC NAME: *Ailuropoda melanoleuca*

RED DATA BOOK: Endangered

AVERAGE FULL-GROWN SIZE:
Head and body length 47.3-59 inches (120-150 cm)
Height at shoulder 27.6-31.5 inches (70-80 cm)

FULL-GROWN WEIGHT:
165-353 pounds (75-160 kg)

LIFE SPAN: 30 years

North America
Atlantic Ocean
Europe
Asia
Africa
Equator
South America
Indian Ocean
Australia
Pacific Ocean

ASIAN ELEPHANT

The Asian elephant is the largest land mammal in Asia. Its habitat is forests, and it used to live across most of southern Asia from Syria and Iraq to China and Indonesia. Today, wild Asian elephants are limited to isolated pockets of their former range, which now excludes all of western Asia. The total wild population is less than forty thousand. There are another fifteen thousand held in captivity, mainly working as beasts of burden in the timber industry.

Asian elephants require a large range to supply enough food. On average, each animal eats about 310 pounds (140 kg) of grasses, including bamboo, bark, roots, and foliage, each day. Crops such as bananas, rice, and sugar cane are also favored. Elephant herds are always on the move in search of food. This frequently brings them into conflict with humans, particularly where the forests are being cleared for agriculture. At one plantation in Indonesia, a herd of elephants destroyed 269,000 rubber saplings in three weeks. Governments throughout the elephant areas in Asia are under pressure to eliminate elephants from around human settlements.

The western populations of the Asian elephant, which are now extinct, were hunted for ivory. Today, elephants are still hunted, but rarely for ivory. Only male Asian elephants have tusks, which are smaller than those of the African elephant, and many males are tuskless. Asian elephants are now hunted for their hides, and in Myanmar alone, fifty elephants are shot and skinned each week.

The Asian elephant was listed as endangered in 1973, and in 1989 the Asian Elephant Conservation Centre was founded in Bangalore. This organization helps to establish protected areas in different countries and creates international corridors for elephant migration. In 1991, the Indian government set up Project Elephant, a conservation program similar to Project Tiger. It is creating elephant reserves so conflict with humans can be minimized.

FACTS

SCIENTIFIC NAME: *Elephas maximus*

RED DATA BOOK: Endangered

AVERAGE FULL-GROWN SIZE:
Head and body length 18 feet (5.5 m)
Tail length 4-5 feet (1.2-1.5 m)
Height at shoulder 8-9.8 feet (2.5-3 m)

FULL-GROWN WEIGHT:
Males 11,907 pounds (5,400 kg); females 6,000 pounds (2,720 kg)

LIFE SPAN: 70 years

Poachers hunt the Asian elephant mainly for its valuable hide.

AFRICAN ELEPHANT

The African elephant is the largest land animal in existence. Although it has been persecuted for centuries for its ivory, only recently has there been concern for its safety. Elephants used to be numerous and widespread throughout Africa south of the Sahara, but they were reduced to 1.3 million by 1980 and 610,000 in 1990. The elephant is extinct in northern Africa, and its distribution is very fragmented elsewhere.

There are two subspecies, the forest elephant of western and central Africa, and the larger savanna or bush elephant, which is the best known and most abundant. African elephants live in herds that consist of groups of related females and their young. Males live alone or in groups that may associate with the female groups. Sometimes groups gather into herds of hundreds or thousands. Elephants are long-lived and slow-breeding. Females are mature at about ten years of age and give birth every three or four years. Their diet consists of vegetation of many kinds, and each group has a large range to travel in search of food.

The demand for ivory has been the elephant's main downfall. The Arab ivory trade made elephants scarce in the seventeenth century, but a great rise in ivory prices during the 1970s, at a time when Africa was flooded with civil wars and modern weapons, started the big decline of the African elephant. National park rangers have been unable to compete with well-armed poachers. Over 80 percent of ivory now comes from poached elephants, and the countries where ivory is illegally imported or exported must work to prevent the trade.

Even if the illegal ivory trade is stopped, the future of the African elephant is bleak. The increasing human population of Africa makes it difficult for elephant herds to find the large areas of country they need. The herds are increasingly confined to national parks. Here they may become so numerous that their numbers sometimes have to be culled to prevent them from destroying the existing vegetation.

Demand for the African elephant's magnificent tusks has been one of the major reasons for its declining numbers.

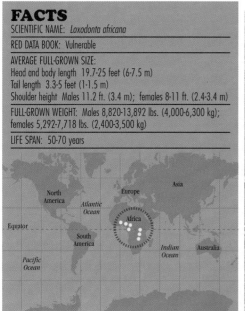

FACTS

SCIENTIFIC NAME: *Loxodonta africana*

RED DATA BOOK: Vulnerable

AVERAGE FULL-GROWN SIZE:
Head and body length 19.7-25 feet (6-7.5 m)
Tail length 3.3-5 feet (1-1.5 m)
Shoulder height Males 11.2 ft. (3.4 m); females 8-11 ft. (2.4-3.4 m)

FULL-GROWN WEIGHT: Males 8,820-13,892 lbs. (4,000-6,300 kg);
females 5,292-7,718 lbs. (2,400-3,500 kg)

LIFE SPAN: 50-70 years

AFRICAN WILD ASS

There may be only a few hundred African wild asses left in existence.

FACTS

SCIENTIFIC NAME: *Equus asinus*

RED DATA BOOK: Endangered

AVERAGE FULL-GROWN SIZE:
Head and body length 6.6 feet (2 m)
Tail length 1.5 feet (.45 m)
Height at shoulder 4 feet (1.25 m)

FULL-GROWN WEIGHT:
550 pounds (250 kg)

LIFE SPAN: Not known

The African wild ass is the animal from which the domestic donkey is descended. It lives in the deserts and dry grasslands and bushlands of Ethiopia from the Danakil Desert into the Ogaden Plateau, Djibouti, and northern Somalia. Previously, its range extended from Morocco to the Sudan and Somalia.

Like other members of the horse family, wild asses graze on grass and other herbs, and they also browse on any leaves, fruits, tree bark, and shrubs they can reach. They can survive for long periods without water in their dry habitat. The stallions defend very large territories, often around water. The mares lead a wandering life and associate with individual stallions for mating. When they have foals, they associate with other females. At other times, asses form unstable herds of up to fifty animals.

At one time, no one knew for certain whether any wild asses survived in Africa. Experts now know that some small populations survive. Optimistic estimates put their numbers at 6,000 to 12,000, but there may be no more than a few hundred. One problem is that wild asses interbreed with domestic asses, or donkeys. Wild asses are also hunted for food, and civil wars in their homeland have provided more humans with access to modern weapons. Their habitat is also taken over by domestic animals that keep the wild asses from water and feeding grounds.

Wild asses are legally protected in Sudan, Somalia, and Ethiopia, but the only protected areas where they live are the Yangudi-Rassa National Park and surrounding wildlife reserves and controlled hunting areas. A population was set up in the Hai-Bar Desert from asses caught in the Danakil Desert. This population reached twenty-six at one time, but breeding and survival are poor, and only eighteen remained in 1992.

GREVY'S ZEBRA

Grevy's zebra is a relative of the better known and more widespread plains zebra of eastern Africa. It lives in the semidesert grassland and scrub country in northern Kenya and Ethiopia. Six thousand years ago, it ranged as far north as Egypt.

Zebras eat coarse vegetation, grazing mainly on grasses and herbs, but they also browse on low shrubs. Grevy's zebra has a loose social life. Most adult males live alone in large territories, where females visit them for mating. Otherwise, females and nonbreeding males live in herds that gather and break up at intervals that depend on environmental conditions.

During the 1970s, hunting for skins was a major threat to Grevy's zebras, but this problem has been solved by placing the species on a list that bans international trade in certain animal products. The zebras are also legally protected in Ethiopia, and there is a hunting ban in Kenya. They are still threatened by changes in their habitat, since they have to compete with increasing numbers of livestock. The situation is made worse by previously nomadic herders that now lead more settled lives around the major water sources and

prevent access to the water for the zebras. Tourism can also be a problem where it is not managed properly. Motor vehicles cause erosion and damage the vegetation. Breeding areas suffer from excessive disturbance, and animals are often prevented from getting to water.

Grevy's zebras inhabit several reserves in Kenya and Ethiopia, and attempts are being made to link reserves with corridors so that the zebras have a larger range in which to live.

FACTS

SCIENTIFIC NAME: *Equus grevyi*

RED DATA BOOK: Endangered

AVERAGE FULL-GROWN SIZE:
Head and body length 8.2-9.8 feet (2.5-3 m)
Tail length 1.2-2 feet (.38-.6 m)

FULL-GROWN WEIGHT:
776-992 pounds (352-450 kg)

LIFE SPAN: 22 years

Grevy's zebras live in semidesert and scrub areas in Kenya and Ethiopia.

MOUNTAIN TAPIR

The mountain tapir is a relative of the Malayan tapir that lives in a very different habitat on the other side of the world. The mountain tapir lives only at high altitudes in the Andes Mountains of Colombia, Ecuador, and Peru. It has never been found below 6,560 feet (2,000 m) and ranges as high as 13,125 feet (4,000 m). At these altitudes, it is so cold and windy that the trees in the mountainous forests are stunted.

Little is known about the habits of the mountain tapir. It is more active at night and lives near streams and wet places, just like its Malayan relative. Small herds of five to seven have been spotted, and usually one calf is born at a time. Mountain tapirs are browsers and grazers that eat ferns and young shoots.

Only a few thousand mountain tapirs remain. A very small population survives in Peru, and the species that once lived in Venezuela is probably extinct now. As well as being hunted, mountain tapirs have suffered from destruction of their mountain habitat through grazing by cattle and expansion of human settlement and farming. There is also a trade in live animals for zoos.

Mountain tapirs are legally protected in the three countries they inhabit, but the law is not strictly enforced. They can be found in protected areas in Colombia and Peru, but more reserves and better protection are needed to save the species.

FACTS

SCIENTIFIC NAME: *Tapirus pinchaque*

RED DATA BOOK: Endangered

AVERAGE FULL-GROWN SIZE:
Head and body length 6 feet (1.8 m)
Height at shoulder 2.5-2.6 feet (.75-.8 m)

FULL-GROWN WEIGHT:
496-550 pounds (225-250 kg)

LIFE SPAN: 24 years

A young mountain tapir photographed in Ecuador.

FACTS

SCIENTIFIC NAME: *Tapirus indicus*

RED DATA BOOK: Endangered

AVERAGE FULL-GROWN SIZE:
Head and body length 8.2 feet (2.5 m)
Height at shoulder 3.3 feet (1 m)

FULL-GROWN WEIGHT:
573-827 pounds (260-375 kg)

LIFE SPAN: 30 years

The Malayan tapir is a distinctive-looking animal.

The black-and-white color and short trunk give the Malayan tapir a unique appearance. It looks as if it is related to the elephants, but its closest relatives are the horses and rhinoceroses.

The Malayan tapir lives in dense, undisturbed rain forests, often near streams and swamps, from Myanmar and Thailand to Malaysia and Sumatra. Although there are occasional reports from Borneo, the tapir has probably not lived there for thousands of years.

Tapirs are browsers and feed on leaves and twigs from the bottom layer of the rain forest. The trunk is used to pull food toward the mouth.

Although common in Myanmar, Malaysia, and Indonesia until fifty years ago, the Malayan tapir is now rare. It is only found in a few remote places or in reserves. The main reason for its decline is the destruction of the rain forests, but tapirs are also hunted for their meat and thick hides for leather goods. However, they are safe in Sumatra and Myanmar because religious reasons prevent them from being killed.

Tapirs are protected by game laws in Myanmar, Thailand, Malaysia, and Indonesia, but the laws are not always strictly enforced. The survival of the Malayan tapir will depend on the preservation of the rain forest where it can live undisturbed.

WHITE RHINOCEROS

There are two subspecies of white rhinoceros that have widely separated ranges. The northern subspecies once lived west of the Nile River in Zaïre, Sudan, and the Central African Republic. The southern subspecies once lived in southern Africa south of the Zambezi River. The present range of both subspecies is very restricted. The northern subspecies is now confined to the Garamba National Park in Zaïre, where thirty-two were living in 1993. There were 6,752 of the southern subspecies at the same time.

The white rhinoceros received its name from the Afrikaans word *wijd*, meaning "wide." This describes the broad square lips that the rhino uses for cropping short grass. The white rhino is more sociable than other species of rhinoceros. Territorial bulls are solitary, but herds of rhinos can sometimes be seen.

The northern subspecies was relatively abundant until the 1970s. It became a victim of the trade in rhinoceros horn to Yemen, where it is used to make dagger handles. Trade has declined since the 1980s, but rhino horn is still used for traditional medicine in eastern Asia. The rhino's survival depends on maintaining defenses against poaching.

The story of the southern subspecies is an example of successful conservation. It was almost exterminated a century ago, and the last population, in the Umfolosi Game Reserve, eventually came under effective protection in 1920. By the 1960s, numbers had risen to nearly two thousand, and Operation Rhino was set up to catch some rhinoceroses and liberate them in other parts of their former range. This has been so successful that the species has been removed from the endangered list.

White rhinoceros conservation in South Africa is a good example of what can be achieved with a species close to extinction.

FACTS

SCIENTIFIC NAME: *Ceratotherium simum*

RED DATA BOOK: Vulnerable

AVERAGE FULL-GROWN SIZE:
Head and body length 11-13.8 feet (3.4-4.2 m)
Tail length 1.6-2.3 feet (.5-.7 m)

FULL-GROWN WEIGHT: Males 4,410-6,615 pounds (2,000-3,000 kg); females 2,205-3750 pounds (1,000-1,700 kg)

LIFE SPAN: 40-50 years

SUMATRAN RHINOCEROS

The Sumatran rhinoceros is the only one of the three Asian rhinoceros species with two horns, and it is also probably the most endangered of all five of the world's rhinoceroses. It lives in virgin rain forests or the secondary growth that has grown up where these have been cut down. Its diet includes leaves, twigs, and sometimes fruit, and some of the rhino's favorite foods are mangoes, figs, and bamboo.

At one time, there was enough rain forest habitat for Sumatran rhinoceroses to live from the foothills of the Himalayas in Bhutan and eastern India through Myanmar, Thailand, and the Malay Peninsula, as well as on the islands of Sumatra and Borneo. It may also have lived in Cambodia, Laos, and Vietnam. As the forests have been cleared, the rhinoceroses continue to survive on mountainsides where logging and clearing have not begun. They are now mainly confined to small pockets of forest in Myanmar, Thailand, the Malay Peninsula,

Sumatra, and Borneo. The present population is about 400 to 500 animals.

Sumatran rhinoceroses are probably solitary except in the breeding season, when females can be spotted with their young. Each rhinoceros has a home range with a salt lick that has been set out by humans. Much of their time is spent wallowing in pools, which they may dig themselves. Experts believe wallowing helps keep the rhinoceroses cool and protects them from biting insects.

Habitat destruction caused the primary decline of the Sumatran rhinoceros, which is now living in populations that may be too small to survive. People hunting for rhinoceros horns that are used for medicines has recently increased the chance that the species will become extinct. Attempts are being made to save it by breeding in captivity.

FACTS

SCIENTIFIC NAME: *Dicerorhinus sumatrensis*

RED DATA BOOK: Endangered

AVERAGE FULL-GROWN SIZE:
Head and body length 7.7-10.4 feet (2.36-3.18 m)
Height at shoulder 3.7-4.8 feet (1.12-1.45 m)

FULL-GROWN WEIGHT:
1,764-4,410 pounds (800-2,000 kg)

LIFE SPAN: over 32 years

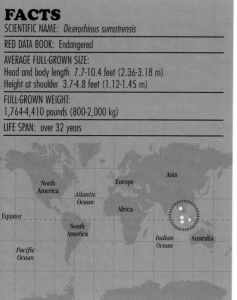

The Sumatran rhinoceros is a solitary creature for most of its life, roaming the territory around its salt lick.

BLACK RHINOCEROS

The black rhinoceros population has fallen by 97 percent in twenty-five years.

Until about twenty-five years ago, the black rhinoceros was still quite common throughout the savanna region of Africa, avoiding only the equatorial forests and deserts. In the 1970s, a dramatic decline set in, and the species is now rare. It survives only in isolated pockets, and many countries have been left with such small populations that the animal cannot survive. The largest populations are in Kenya, Namibia, Zimbabwe, and South Africa. The total population is 2,550, about 900 of which live in South Africa.

The black rhinoceros is generally solitary, although groups may gather at wallows. It feeds by browsing on leaves and new twigs, especially those of acacia trees.

Black rhinoceroses have been hunted for several reasons: for sport, because they are considered dangerous, and for their thick hides. When Asian rhinoceroses became rare, the black rhinoceroses began to be hunted for their horns, which are used in Asian medicines. In the 1970s, there was a sudden increase in demand for rhino horns in North Yemen, where they are traditionally used for dagger handles. Previously, few Yemenis could afford rhino horns, but the situation changed when they began to earn high wages in Saudi Arabia and other oil-rich states. The price of horn soared during the 1970s, and poaching rhinoceroses became very profitable. The population of black rhinoceroses decreased by 97 percent between 1970 and 1994.

The Conservation Action Plan is trying to stop the trade in rhino horns by applying political pressure on governments to stop illegal import and export. It also encourages the use of substitute materials and tries to protect black rhinos in the wild. One method of discouraging poachers, which is used in Namibia, Zimbabwe, and Swaziland, is to saw off the horns of living rhinos so poachers will leave the animals alone.

JAVAN RHINOCEROS

The Javan rhinoceros was once widespread throughout southeastern Asia from Bengal eastward through Myanmar, Thailand, Laos, and Vietnam and south to Malaysia, Sumatra, and Java. It is now probably the rarest large mammal in the world. It is restricted to the Ujung Kulon National Park in Java, where there are fifty to sixty rhinoceroses, and a small population of eight to twelve animals discovered in Vietnam in 1992.

Javan rhinos live in low-lying, dense rain forests with plenty of water and mud wallows. Their food is foliage, twigs, and fallen fruit. They are very elusive as well as rare. They are solitary except when courting and when mothers are accompanied by their single offspring.

The loss of rain forest has been most severe at the low altitudes preferred by Javan rhinoceroses, and large areas of southeastern Asia are now uninhabitable. Their plight has been made worse by the demand for rhinoceros horn and other parts of the body that are used for local medicines.

The tiny populations that remain are very vulnerable to poaching. They could also easily be destroyed by a natural disaster or disease, and inbreeding could cause genetic problems.

The Javan Rhinoceros Action Plan focuses on the Ujong Kulon population, which is the most viable population. The plan will survey the park to determine the precise habitat requirements of the species and the resources needed to protect it. Captive breeding will be attempted. In Vietnam, a search is planned to locate more rhinos.

FACTS

SCIENTIFIC NAME: *Rhinoceros sondaicus*

RED DATA BOOK: Endangered

AVERAGE FULL-GROWN SIZE:
Head and body length 9.8-10.5 feet (3-3.2 m)
Tail length 2.3 feet (.7 m)

FULL-GROWN WEIGHT:
3,308-4,410 pounds (1,500 - 2,000 kg)

LIFE SPAN: 21 years

A rare photo of the elusive Javan rhinoceros. The total number left in the wild is probably less than seventy-five.

GREAT INDIAN RHINOCEROS

The great Indian rhinoceros once lived across the northern part of the Indian subcontinent, from Pakistan in the west to the Indian-Myanmar border and including parts of Nepal and Bhutan. It may also have existed in Myanmar, southern China, and Indochina. It now exists in a few small populations on the northern border of eastern India and Nepal. The surviving population is just under 1,900 animals.

The habitat of the great Indian rhinoceros is flat river plains, where the grass grows to 26 feet (8 m), and adjacent swamps and forests. This habitat has been very suitable for human settlement, and the plains have been converted into cropland, pasture, and plantations. As the natural habitat has decreased, the rhinoceroses have been forced into cultivated areas and into increased conflict with humans. Several humans are killed each year by rhinos. This situation has also made the rhinoceroses more accessible to hunters.

Hunting for sport became popular with both Europeans and Asians in the nineteenth and early twentieth centuries. A government bounty to protect tea plantations in Assam from rhinoceros damage also had a major effect on the total numbers. By the first decade of the twentieth century, the great Indian rhinoceros was almost extinct. The main group of survivors consisted of twelve individuals in one area of Assam.

Persecution continues and is increasing because of the market demand for rhino products used in traditional medicines. Five percent are poached each year in Assam, where most of the surviving rhinos live. This equals the growth rate of the population, so numbers are likely to continue declining.

The great Indian rhinoceros is protected in India and Nepal. The Asian Rhino Action Plan has the objective of maintaining a wild population of 2,000 rhinoceroses in six or more reserves in India and Nepal. The animals' survival depends on a reduction in poaching.

Less than two thousand great Indian rhinoceroses remain in the wild.

FACTS

SCIENTIFIC NAME: *Rhinoceros unicornis*

RED DATA BOOK: Endangered

AVERAGE FULL-GROWN SIZE:
Head and body length Males 12-12.5 feet (3.7–3.8 m);
females 10-11 feet (3.1-3.4 m)
Tail length 2.3-2.6 feet (.7-.8 m)
Height at shoulder Males 5.6-6.2 feet (1.7-1.9 m)
females 4.9-5.6 feet (1.5-1.7 m)

WEIGHT: Males 4,851 lbs. (2,200 kg); females 3,528 lbs. (1,600 kg)

LIFE SPAN: 47 years

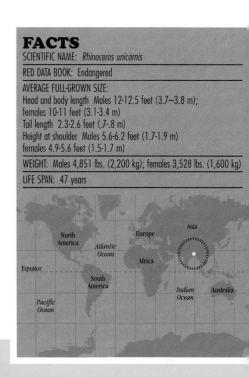

PYGMY HOG

The pygmy hog was once found all along the rivers that ran south of the Himalayan foothills from Uttar Pradesh through Nepal and Bengal to Assam and Bhutan. It is now known to survive only in two reserves in Assam. There are thought to be a few hundred pygmy hogs in the Manas Wildlife Sanctuary and perhaps fewer than fifty in the small Barnadi Wildlife Sanctuary.

The habitat of the pygmy hog is dense, tall grassland with a few trees and shrubs. It lives in small family groups and feeds mainly on roots and tubers that are grubbed out of the ground. At times, the hog also eats small animals.

The low-lying, riverside grasslands where pygmy hogs live are used for agriculture and are often flooded when dams are built. The remaining grasslands are threatened by grazing and forestry. The grass is also used for thatching. The grasslands are regularly burned each dry season so there will be a better crop of grass the following year. This practice deprives the hogs of food and cover, so the animals are much easier to hunt.

The important Manas Wildlife Sanctuary was threatened by a proposal to build two dams in neighboring Bhutan, but protests caused this plan to be abandoned. Armed extremists then took over the sanctuary, killing guards and destroying property.

The pygmy hog has the maximum protection permitted under Indian law, but because of the lawlessness in northwestern Assam, it is impossible to maintain proper protection for the animals.

The pygmy hog's habitat has been destroyed by human activities. It can now be found in only two reserves.

FACTS

SCIENTIFIC NAME: *Suss salvanius*

RED DATA BOOK: Endangered

AVERAGE FULL-GROWN SIZE:
Head and body length 25.6 inches (65 cm)
Tail length 9.85 inches (25 cm)

FULL-GROWN WEIGHT:
18.7 pounds (8.5 kg)

LIFE SPAN: Not known

The Siberian musk deer lives in eastern Siberia, east of the Yensei River and Altai Mountains, and also in northern Mongolia, Manchuria, and Korea. Its habitat is forest and brushlands at heights of 8,530 to 11,810 feet (2,600 to 3,600 m). It is shy, usually solitary, and nocturnal, and it spends its days asleep in dense cover. The deer's diet consists of grasses, mosses, lichens, and shoots.

The numbers of musk deer are difficult to estimate because of their shy habits. They used to be abundant, but the population has declined rapidly in recent years because of habitat destruction and hunting. The population of musk deer in Russia is estimated to have dropped by 70 percent in two or three years, and the animal may become extinct there in just a few years.

Siberian musk deer are hunted for the musk glands of the male. The brownish, waxy secretions from the glands are used by the deer for marking their territories. The secretions are highly valued for making perfume, soap, and medicines and command a price of up to $20,000 per pound ($45,000 per kg). Because one deer provides only about 1 ounce (30 g) of musk, it is not surprising that huge numbers of deer are killed. The females and young do not produce musk, but they are often killed in traps set for the males.

Most of the musk goes to the Republic of Korea, where it is used in the multimillion dollar manufacture of Hwang Chung Shim Won medicine balls used in most Korean homes. Seven hundred pounds (317 kg), valued at $4.7 million, were imported into the Republic of Korea in 1992.

Siberian musk deer are protected in many places, and the trade in musk is regulated, but these measures are not enough to save the species. Captive farming of musk deer has been tried in China and Russia, but these schemes probably encourage the demand for musk and thus promote hunting.

FACTS

SCIENTIFIC NAME: *Moschus moschiferus*

RED DATA BOOK: Endangered

AVERAGE FULL-GROWN SIZE:
Head and body length 31.5-39.4 inches (80-100 cm)
Tail length 19.7-29.6 inches (50-75 cm)

FULL-GROWN WEIGHT:
15.4-37.5 pounds (7-17 kg)

LIFE SPAN: 20 years

A rare photograph of the very shy Siberian musk deer.

PÈRE DAVID'S DEER

Père David's deer had been extinct in the wild. However, in 1985, a small herd was released into its original habitat. Père David's deer originally lived in the lowlands of eastern China, probably in the reed beds of swampy marshlands. It was hunted extensively and probably became extinct in the wild more than three hundred years ago.

Père David's deer are grazers that feed on grass and water plants in summer. They live in herds, and the males gather harems of females in the breeding season.

Some Père David's deer survived in the Imperial Hunting Park, south of Beijing. A missionary, Abbé Armand David, obtained two skins in 1865 by bribing the park guards. These specimens were the first knowledge that western scientists had of the species. Later, several live deer were sent to zoos in Europe. In 1894, most of the imperial herd drowned in a flood, and the remainder were hunted in a famine and during the Boxer Rebellion. The last member of the herd died in Beijing Zoo in 1922. However, a herd was built up in a private zoo at Woburn, England, which now numbers six hundred deer, and there are about 150 collections of Père David's deer around the world. They are all descended from the original eighteen deer at Woburn. In 1956, some of Père David's deer were returned to Beijing, and in 1985 they were reintroduced to the wild. China now has two wild herds of Père David's deer, with a combined total of about 170 deer.

FACTS

SCIENTIFIC NAME: *Elaphurus davidianus*

RED DATA BOOK: Endangered

AVERAGE FULL-GROWN SIZE:
Head and body length 5.9-7 feet (1.8-2.2 m)
Tail length .72-1.2 feet (.22-.36 m)
Height at shoulder 4-4.5 feet (1.22-1.37 m)

FULL-GROWN WEIGHT:
Males 472 pounds (214 kg); females 350 pounds (159 kg)

LIFE SPAN: 23 years

The Père David's deer was rescued from extinction by a group of concerned people at Woburn Park in England.

WILD YAK

Wild yaks are endangered mainly because of hunting and competition from domestic yaks.

One hundred years ago, there were huge herds of wild yaks in the high mountain plateaus of Tibet and adjacent parts of China, India, and possibly Bhutan. Today, there are only a few hundred left. There are, however, as many as twelve million domestic yaks, which are about half the size of wild yaks. Domestic yaks are important animals for mountain people. They have been used as beasts of burden and have provided meat, milk, and wool for over two thousand years.

The home of the wild yak is the steppes and tundras at heights of 13,125 to 16,400 feet (4,000 to 5,000 m) or even higher. The yaks survive the cold winters with the help of their long, dense coats. Summer is spent high in the mountains where there is permanent snow, and the rest of the year is spent lower down. Yaks look clumsy, but they are sure-footed and good climbers. The cows and their calves live in herds, once numbering thousands, while the bulls live in groups of two or three. A single calf is born every other year.

Wild yaks have become rare because of uncontrolled hunting. They are also threatened by domestic yaks that compete for food and may spread disease to the wild population. The wild stock is also threatened by interbreeding with domestic animals. Yet wild yaks are important for breeding with domestic yaks as a means of improving the breed.

Legal protection is difficult to enforce in remote mountain regions. Programs have been set up in China and India, however, to conserve wild yaks by locating the wild herds and setting up reserves. Captive breeding is also needed.

The markhor is the largest wild goat in the world. The male has curved horns measuring 32-56 inches (82-143 cm). It lives in mountain ranges, usually around the level of the tree line at 2,295-13,125 feet (700-4,000 m). It mainly inhabits woods, but it is also found in rocky gorges and alpine meadows.

At one time, markhors ranged across the mountainous parts of central Asia, in Afghanistan, northern Pakistan and India, Uzbekistan, Turkmenistan, and Tajikistan. They are probably now extinct in Afghanistan and are reduced to small, isolated populations elsewhere. There are probably only a few thousand left.

Adult male markhors usually live alone and associate with the herds of females and young only in the mating season. The herds are usually small, but sometimes up to one hundred markhors gather together. They are mainly grazers that feed on grass in spring and summer. When the grasses have dried up in the summer heat, the markhors turn to browsing on the leaves and twigs of shrubs such as sea buckthorn and holly oak.

The large horns of the markhor have always made it a highly valued trophy species. The horns have also been used in traditional medicines and, in China, horns have been reported selling recently for $450 per pound ($1,000 per kg). Markhors are particularly vulnerable in winter, when they descend to more accessible slopes. Local people need fresh meat at this time, and they have modern weapons because of the wars in Afghanistan and elsewhere. Many local populations of markhors have been exterminated for these reasons. Because the rocky habitat is discontinuous, it is very difficult for the markhor to recolonize naturally. Remaining populations are also at risk from competition for food from domestic goats and other animals.

There is an urgent need for properly protected reserves for markhors. The 220 markhors in captivity in 1992 produced 100 young in 1991, so there is the possibility of reintroducing the species to the wild.

FACTS

SCIENTIFIC NAME: *Capra falconi*

RED DATA BOOK: Endangered

AVERAGE FULL-GROWN SIZE:
Head and body length 4.6-5.9 feet (1.4-1.8 m)
Shoulder height 2-3.4 feet (.65-1.04 m)

FULL-GROWN WEIGHT: Males 176-243 pounds (80-110 kg); females 70-88 pounds (32-40 kg)

LIFE SPAN: 12 years

A male markhor displays its distinctive curved horns.

ARABIAN ORYX

The long horns of the Arabian oryx may be the origin of the unicorn legend. The species once inhabited the dry gravel plains and sandy deserts of the Arabian Peninsula northward into Israel, Jordan, Iraq, Syria, and the Sinai Peninsula of Egypt.

The habitat of the Arabian oryx is one of the harshest in the world. The vegetation is very scattered, and the oryx must keep moving in search of food. It grazes on grass and herbs and also eats the leaves, seedpods, roots, and tubers of acacia trees. Like other desert mammals, it rarely needs to drink. Arabian oryxes live in groups of up to twenty, which are composed of all ages and both sexes.

The Arabian oryx began to disappear in the middle of the nineteenth century. By the outbreak of World War I, few remained outside Saudi Arabia. After World War II, the spread of modern firearms and efficient motor vehicles made hunting the oryx much easier. By the 1960s, it survived in only two small areas: where the borders of Saudi Arabia, Yemen, and Oman meet and in northeastern Oman. The last wild Arabian oryx was probably killed in 1972.

In 1962, Operation Oryx was set up by the Fauna Preservation Society (now Fauna and Flora Preservation Society). Three wild animals were captured and taken to Phoenix Zoo in Arizona, where, with six captive animals, they formed the World Herd. By 1984, there were over two hundred oryxes in captivity. In 1974, the White Oryx Project was launched to return the species to the wild. The first herd of ten was released in Oman in 1982, and their numbers had increased to 175 in 1993. They are guarded by locally recruited rangers, and tribespeople have agreed not to graze their cattle in the area. Arabian oryx have also been released in Jordan, and there are plans to reintroduce the animals in Saudi Arabia, Syria, and Israel.

FACTS

SCIENTIFIC NAME: *Oryx leucoryx*

RED DATA BOOK: Endangered

AVERAGE FULL-GROWN SIZE:
Head and body length 65 inches (165 cm)
Shoulder height 33 inches (84 cm)

FULL-GROWN WEIGHT:
220-463 pounds (100-210 kg)

LIFE SPAN: 20 years

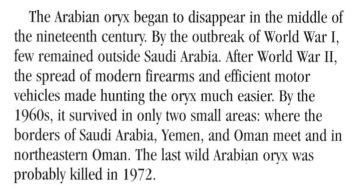

The Arabian oryx became extinct in the wild in the 1970s, but the White Oryx Project has successfully reestablished the breed in Oman.

VU QUANG OX

In May 1992, a party of zoologists surveying the Vu Quang Nature Reserve in Vietnam near its border with Laos discovered three sets of horns belonging to an oxlike animal in the houses of hunters. The long, straight horns showed they belonged to an animal unknown to science. One specimen was obviously fresh because it contained maggots. This was the first discovery of a new large mammal since the okapi was discovered in the forests of Zaïre in 1910.

Although the Vu Quang ox was new to science, it was known to local people who called it Sao La – spindle horn, or Son Duong – mountain goat. More visits to the area have shown that the ox is probably restricted to an area of 1,500 square miles (4,000 sq. km) along the Vietnam-Laos border, in the Annamite Mountains to the south of the Song Ca River. Its habitat is pristine forests of conifers and evergreen broad-leaved trees. It stays in high ground in summer and comes to lower levels in winter. It is a browser that eats the leaves of figs and other bushes.

The species is very shy, living in small groups of two or three, rarely up to six or seven, and it does not enter agricultural land.

The population in Vietnam is estimated to be only a few hundred animals. As soon as it was discovered, the Vietnamese Ministry of Forestry enlarged the Vu Quang Nature Reserve and cancelled logging in the area. Other reserves are being planned in Vietnam and Laos, and local people are being informed of the importance of the Vu Quang ox so they will stop hunting it. In 1994, another survey showed that the ox also lived in the part of Laos that borders the known range in Vietnam. A reserve that adjoins the Vu Quang Nature Reserve is being enlarged to cover more of the Vu Quang ox's natural habitat.

The Vu Quang ox was first discovered in 1992 in the forests of Vietnam.

FACTS

SCIENTIFIC NAME: *Pseudoryx nghetinensis*

RED DATA BOOK: Endangered

AVERAGE FULL-GROWN SIZE:
Head and body length 5 feet (1.5 m)
Height at shoulder 2.6-3 feet (.8-.9 m)

FULL-GROWN WEIGHT:
220 pounds (100 kg)

LIFE SPAN: Unknown

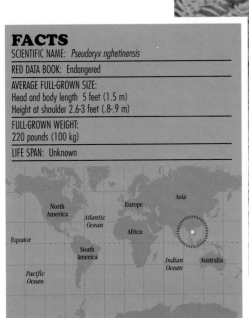

SALT MARSH HARVEST MOUSE

FACTS

SCIENTIFIC NAME: *Reithrodontomys raviventris*

RED DATA BOOK: Endangered

AVERAGE FULL-GROWN SIZE:
Total body length 4.7-6.9 inches (118-175 mm)

FULL-GROWN WEIGHT:
.3 ounces (9 g)

LIFE SPAN: Not known

The salt marsh harvest mouse can only be found around San Francisco Bay.

The salt marsh harvest mouse survives on very salty food and water. It lives in salt marshes that are flooded by the sea every day at high tide, and it is found only in marshes around San Francisco Bay in California.

Little is known about the life-style of the salt marsh harvest mouse. It is a solitary animal that is active mainly by night, and it rarely ventures outside the dense cover of the salt marsh vegetation. It can swim well, and its fur does not get waterlogged as easily as that of related harvest mice. Its diet consists of the stems and leaves of salt marsh plants with a few seeds and insects.

The salt marsh habitat was once continuous around San Francisco Bay, but it has been destroyed by urban land development and drainage. Only 20 percent of the original marshes now survive, and pressure to build houses and an airport threatens the remainder.

There are less than two thousand salt marsh harvest mice left, and their survival depends on a recovery plan. The marshes that are protected need to be enlarged and linked to make large areas of habitat. Some marshes also need improvement because they are managed for wildfowl by growing one kind of plant that is not suitable for the mice. The landward edge of many marshes has also been built up so that the mice do not have a refuge at high tide.

AMAMI RABBIT

The Amami rabbit is a living fossil because it has similarities to fossil rabbits that lived during the Miocene Era. It now lives only on Amami Oshima and Tokuno-shima, two islands of the Ryukyu Archipelago at the southern end of Japan.

The habitat of the Amami rabbit is forest; it does not survive in farmland or residential areas. It eats Japanese pampas grass, Japanese sweet potato, the acorns of the pasania tree, and the bark of various forest trees. It lives in burrows, where litters of one to three young are born twice a year. When above ground, it uses a series of runs through the undergrowth.

The two islands have suffered from extensive logging, which has reduced the area of old forest to 5 percent of the area that existed in 1980. Although the rabbit will probably colonize new growths of secondary forest, preservation of the old forests will be essential for preserving the species. The species was traditionally hunted for medicinal purposes, but it has been declared a National Monument by the Japanese government and given legal protection from shooting and trapping. Feral dogs and cats are its main predators. Conservationists suggest that removing these animals will be critical for saving the Amami rabbit. It has been estimated that 3,750 rabbits survive on Amami Oshima and probably less than 500 on Tokuno-shima.

FACTS

SCIENTIFIC NAME: *Pentalagus furnessi*

RED DATA BOOK: Endangered

AVERAGE FULL-GROWN SIZE:
Head and body length 17-20 inches (43-51 cm)

FULL-GROWN WEIGHT:
4.4-6.6 pounds (2-3 kg)

LIFE SPAN: Not known

The Amami rabbit is a rare living fossil.

VOLCANO RABBIT

The volcano rabbit, the world's smallest rabbit, lives only in a small area of Mexico.

The volcano rabbit is the smallest of all rabbits. It has short ears and a tiny tail. Its only home is on the slopes of four volcanoes — Popocatepetl, Iztaccihuatl, El Pelado, and Tlaloc — in mountain ranges near Mexico City. There are pine forests at heights of 9,185 to 13,945 feet (2,800 to 4,250 m) on the sides of the volcanoes, where the rabbits live under the trees in a habitat of dense clumps of grasses called *zacaton*.

Not much is known about the habits of volcano rabbits. Experts learn only from watching them in zoos. The rabbits live in small groups and are aggressive toward each other. The clumps of zacaton grasses provide places where rabbits can hide from their aggressive neighbors. They are mainly active by day and are very noisy. The females give birth to two babies between December and July.

Volcano rabbits have never been known to live anywhere but on the four volcanoes. This habitat was sufficient for them to be safe until it started to disappear. The pine forests are burned and the grasses are eaten by sheep and cattle or cut for thatching houses. Many fires are started to burn the zacaton to promote fresh growth for domestic animals to eat. The rabbits are also hunted for meat. Conservationists are hoping to persuade local people to leave the volcano rabbit and its habitat alone. Many people do not even realize that it is a protected animal. Conservationists are also trying to regrow the pine forests and the zacaton grasses so there will be more habitat for the volcano rabbit.

FACTS

SCIENTIFIC NAME: *Romerolagus diazi*

RED DATA BOOK: Endangered

AVERAGE FULL-GROWN SIZE:
Total body length 10.6-12.6 inches (27-32 cm)

FULL-GROWN WEIGHT:
17.7 ounces (500 g)

LIFE SPAN: At least 2 years

alpine — of or relating to high mountains or alps.

birds — warm-blooded animals that lay eggs and have feathers and wings.

breed — to mate a male and female animal together for the purpose of producing offspring.

burrows — holes that animals dig in the ground for shelter.

carnivores — flesh-eating animals.

carrion — the dead, often rotting, flesh of animals used as food by other animals.

conservation — the act of preserving animals, plants, or other resources from extinction.

coypu — an aquatic rodent also known as the nutria.

deciduous — falling off or shedding periodically, according to seasonal changes; i.e. leaves.

deforestation — the process of cutting down or clearing forests.

desert — a dry environment, usually sandy, that supports only a few plants and animals.

domestic — tame; kept as a farm animal or pet.

dominant — the animal(s) with the most influence or control in a pack or group.

drought — a period of time with very little or no rain.

durians — large, oval fruits from an East Indian tree.

endangered — at risk of dying out completely, or becoming extinct.

enforce — to make people obey a rule.

equatorial — relating to the area of Earth around the equator.

evergreen — plants with leaves or needles that stay green throughout the year.

export — to ship items to another country for sale.

extinct — no longer existing or living.

flee — to escape.

fossils — the remains of prehistoric animals or plants preserved in rock.

grubs — young insects.

habitat — the natural home of an animal or plant.

hybrid — the product of interbreeding different species of animals or plants.

Iberia — the region of Europe that includes Spain and Portugal.

incubate — to keep a newborn baby warm and safe while it develops.

insulation — protection from the elements, such as extreme cold or heat.

interbreeding — mating between animals or plants of similar species.

invertebrates — animals such as worms, clams, and insects that do not have a backbone.

ivory — the hard, off-white substance of the tusks of elephants and walruses.

litchis — the oval fruits from a tree in the soapberry family.

litter — a number of animals born at the same time to the same mother.

livestock — various types of animals that are raised on farms and ranches.

mammals — warm-blooded animals that feed their young with mother's milk.

mangrove — a tropical tree that lives in a waterlogged, salty environment.

marsupials — mammals, such as kangaroos and wallabies, whose young are born not fully developed, and that complete development in a pouch on the mother's belly.

monogamous — having only one mate at a time.

native — originating or occurring naturally in a region or other particular place.

nocturnal — active only during the night.

offspring — the young produced by a pair of animals.

packs — groups of similar or related animals.

pastures — grassland areas suitable for grazing livestock.

pelts — the skins and fur of dead animals.

plantations — large estates that grow a single crop.

poaching — the illegal catching of animals, usually for profit.

pouch — the baglike part of an animal's body that is used for carrying young offspring.

prairie — a grassy plain with no trees.

predators — animals that kill and eat other animals.

prey — the animals on which another animal feeds.

refugees — people who have escaped from a dangerous place in order to find safety elsewhere.

remains — objects that are left behind.

reserves — areas of land set aside for the protection of wildlife.

roost — a perch or other place where birds or other animals rest. Also the name for a group of resting birds.

salt marsh — an area of soft, wet land near the sea that floods at high tide.

savanna — an environment of grassy plains with clumps of trees.

scrub — an environment consisting mainly of stunted trees and shrubs.

solitary — living alone.

species — a group of animals or plants that breeds with each other, but does not breed with animals or plants outside the group.

superstitions — strong beliefs that actions taken will have profound effects on the outcome of events.

swamp — an area of muddy land that is often filled with water.

terrain — an area of land.

timber — lumber or wood that is used for building.

tonic — a medicine that is believed to provide strength and energy.

tropical — of or relating to the warm, humid area of Earth near the equator. The tropics are the areas of our planet that lie between the Tropic of Cancer and the Tropic of Capricorn.

tundra — a barren environment in which the subsoil is permanently frozen.

viable — (a population) large enough to continue breeding and existing.

zoologists — scientists who study animals.

All Wild Creatures Welcome: The Story of a Wildlife Rehabilitation Center. Patricia Curtis (Lodestar)
The Californian Wildlife Region. V. Brown and G. Lawrence (Naturegraph)
Close to Extinction. John Burton (Watts)
Conservation Directory. (National Wildlife Federation)
Conservation from A to Z. I. Green (Oddo)
Discovering Birds of Prey. Mike Thomas and Eric Soothill (Watts)
Discovering Endangered Species (Nature Discovery Library). Nancy Field and Sally Machlas
    (Dog Eared Publications)
Ecology Basics. Lawrence Stevens (Prentice Hall)
Endangered Animals. John B. Wexo (Creative Education)
Endangered Forest Animals. Dave Taylor (Crabtree)
Endangered Grassland Animals. Dave Taylor (Crabtree)
Endangered Mountain Animals. Dave Taylor (Crabtree)
Endangered Wetland Animals. Dave Taylor (Crabtree)
Endangered Species. Don Lynch (Grace Dangberg Foundation)
Endangered Species Means There's Still Time. (U.S. Government Printing Office, Washington, D.C.)
Endangered Wildlife. M. Banks (Rourke)
Fifty Simple Things Kids Can Do to Save the Earth. Earthworks Group (Andrews and McMeel)
Heroes of Conservation. C. B. Squire (Fleet)
In Peril (4 volumes). Barbara J. Behm and Jean-Christophe Balouet (Gareth Stevens)
Lost Wide Worlds. Robert M. McClung (William Morrow)
Macmillan Children's Guide to Endangered Animals. Roger Few (Macmillan)
Meant to Be Wild. Jan DeBlieu (Fulcrum)
Mountain Gorillas in Danger. Rita Ritchie (Gareth Stevens)
National Wildlife Federation's Book of Endangered Species. Earthbooks, Inc. Staff (Earthbooks, Inc.)
Project Panda Watch. Miriam Schlein (Atheneum)
Save the Earth. Betty Miles (Knopf)
Saving Animals: The World Wildlife Book of Conservation. Bernard Stonehouse (Macmillan)
Why Are Animals Endangered? Isaac Asimov (Gareth Stevens)
Wildlife Alert. Gene S. Stuart (National Geographic)
Wildlife of Cactus and Canyon Country. Marjorie Dunmire (Pegasus)
Wildlife of the Northern Rocky Mountains. William Baker (Naturegraph)

VIDEOS

African Wildlife. (National Geographic)
The Amazing Marsupials. (National Geographic)
Animals Are Beautiful People. Jamie Uys (Pro Footage Library: America's Wildlife)
How to Save Planet Earth. (Pro Footage Library: America's Wildlife)
Predators of the Wild. (Time Warner Entertainment)
Wildlife of Alaska. (Pro Footage Library: America's Wildlife)

INDEX

PICTURE CREDITS

Page 9, Dr Petocz/WWF;
Page 10, © Dean Lee/The Wildlife Collection;
Page 11, Frédy Mercay/WWF;
Page 12, Professor Hidetoshi Ota;
Page 13, G. Anderson/Nature Focus;
Page 14, Jose Luis Gonzalez Grande/Bruce Coleman Ltd;
Page 15, Konrad Wothe/Bruce Coleman Ltd;
Page 16, 17, David Haring/OSF;
Page 18, © John Giustina/The Wildlife Collection;
Page 19, Luiz Claudio Marigo/Bruce Coleman Ltd;
Page 20, Zig Leszczynski/Animals Animals/OSF;
Page 21, John Chellman/Animals Animals/OSF;
Page 22, © Washington Park Zoo/Ellis Nature Photography;
Page 23, Isaac Kehimkar/Dinodia/SOF;
Page 24, Andrew Plumtre/OSF;

Page 25, Michael Leach/OSF;
Page 26, Michel Gunther/WWF;
Page 27, H.D. Rijksen/WWF;
Page 28, Petra Wegner/Foto Natura/WWF;
Page 29, James H. Robinson/OSF;
Page 30, Martin Nicoll/WWF;
Pages 31, 41, M & C Denis-Huot/BIOS/WWF;
Page 32, Fritz Vollmar/WWF;
Page 33, Alan & Sandy Carey/OSF;
Page 34 & front cover Martin Harvey/WWF;
Pages 35, 44, Martin Harvey/Wildlife GmbH/WWF;
Page 36, Tim Campbell/WWF;
Page 37, G. Schulz/Wildlife GmbH/WWF;
Page 38, E. Hanumantha Rao/WWF;
Page 39, Mark Boulton/WWF;
Pages 40, 54, Cyril Ruoso/BIOS/WWF;
Page 42, Juan Pratginestos/WWF;
Page 43, AJT Johnsingh/WWF;

Pages 45, 51, Rod Williams/Bruce Coleman Ltd;
Page 46, S. Cedola/Panda Photos/WWF;
Page 47, Nico J Van Strien/WWF;
Page 48, Daniel Aubort/WWF;
Page 49, Gerald Cubitt/WWF;
Page 50, © Vivek R Sinha/The Wildlife Collection;
Page 52, © John Giustina/The Wildlife Collection;
Page 53, © Bruce Coleman;
Page 55, David Hulse/WWF;
Page 56, Jeff Foott Productions/Bruce Coleman Ltd;
Pages 57, 58, John Harris/Survival/OSF

WWF = World Wide Fund for Nature
OSF = Oxford Scientific Films